The Mentor
Paul Gilbert

Chloe and Olivia
with all my love, Dad x

Published by: LBC Wise Counsel

ISBN 9781838358945

Copyright © 2024 Paul Gilbert

All rights reserved. No part of this publication may be reproduced, stored in a retrieval system, or transmitted, in any form or by any means without the prior permission in writing of the publisher.

This book is sold subject to the condition that it shall not, by way of trade or otherwise, be lent, resold, hired out or otherwise circulated without the publisher's prior consent in any form other than that supplied by the publisher.

British Library Cataloguing in Publication Data available.

CONTENTS

0

Introduction

01 A man called Lawrence 11
02 Give me ten minutes 17
03 United I fell 23
04 This is how it starts 29
05 We are all passing through 37
06 How Ian McKellen and Linda Loman changed my life 41
07 The Yellow House 49
08 From Badlands to bright lights 55
09 Giving it up 63

1

10 Now what? 67
11 The gift of space and time 73
12 Leadership is about love 77
13 Perhaps there isn't an answer dear 85
14 Our beautiful bag of gifts and talents 91
15 When the frame is more important than the picture 97
16 A note of thanks 103
17 For good 107
18 For the stories 115
19 No one ever says "Ray who?" 121

2

20 The Pause 127
21 The rage room 131
22 The Blessings Room 137
23 The rooms beyond blessings Part One 143
24 The rooms beyond blessings Part Two 149
25 Nearly there 153
26 The last chapter, back to the beginning 161

Acknowledgements and thanks 168
Index of images 170

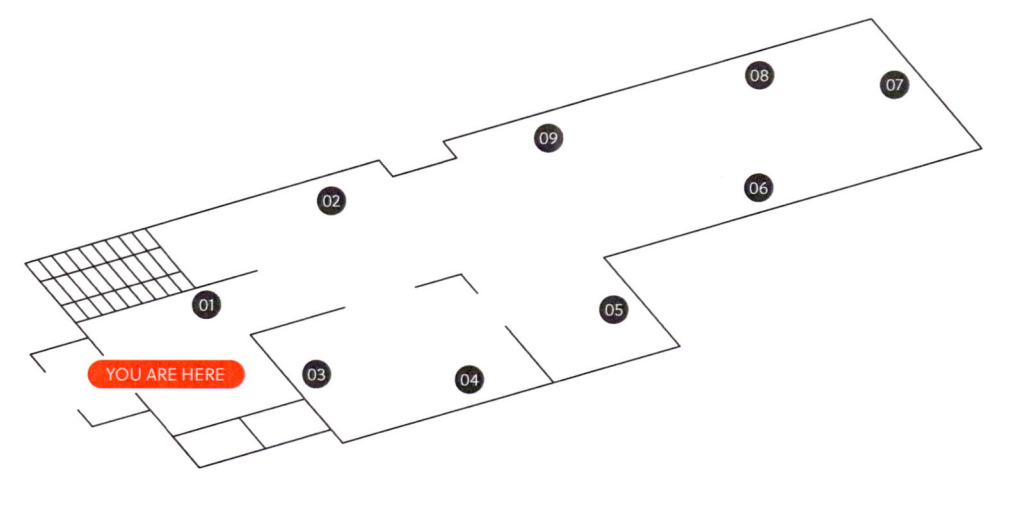
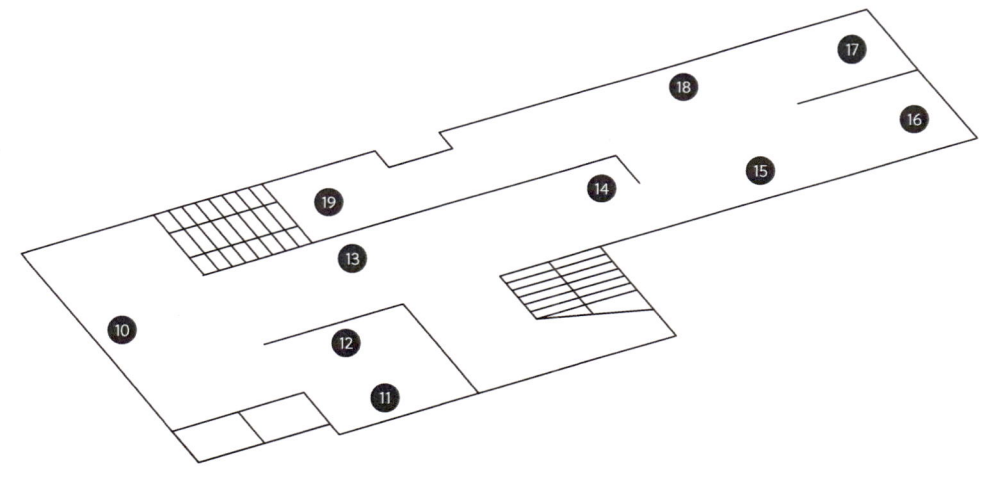
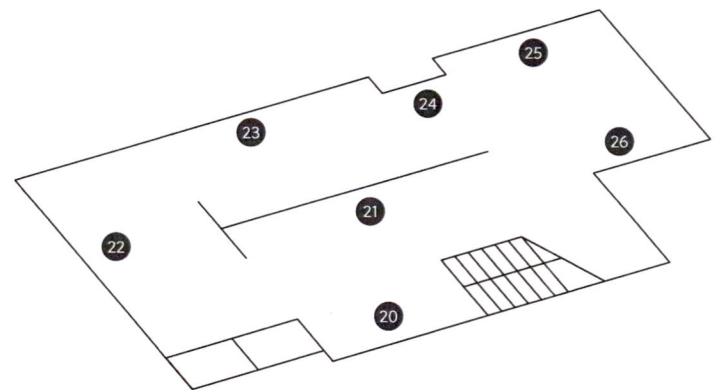

INTRODUCTION

It is the greatest unexplored gift that we possess, but its value is only shown when we share it with others.

Its potential is in every word, deed and reflection. Its shape is formed only when we accept that we influence the lives of everyone we meet. It gains its power when we share it intentionally. It defines its meaning in the difference we make.

It is a gift that we must first cherish for ourselves because in order to share it, we must first be open to its gentle persuasion. If we take it for granted, it weakens into nothing more than tinselled platitudes; but if we honour its kindness and power its impact will be profound and long lasting.

We live in times and in places where everything rushes by, but if we always respond by trying to keep up with the giddying swirl, only exhaustion awaits. If we allow ourselves to pause and to notice, then it is possible that we may see how everything speaks to us and how everything reacts with us. When we share what has touched us, this is how we become the mentor we are meant to be.

In the unfolding story of our time together in the pages that follow, i will share a little of my journey with you, a journey that has been more than sixty years in the making. There is no plot to spoil, no cliff-hanger to lean over and nor is this story about a destination. We do not have to arrive, we just need to be.

In each chapter of our time together, we will pause for a few minutes with thoughts and reflections that briefly take us away from our ever-faster realties. The words we will share will be part memoire, part observation and part reflection. I am not sure what we will discover, but I am certain that if we walk together with a kind thought and an open heart, then we will find meaning for ourselves and for those we care about at home and in our work.

This is the story of a mentor. It is partly my story, but far more importantly it is the story of each of us when we search for meaning and hope that we are good enough to be ourselves.

These may be my words, but they will be your reflections in your world; please hold them dear and let them be your guide. The gift is what you then do with them.

01 A MAN CALLED LAWRENCE

Age is a funny thing. We kind of know that it doesn't really matter; after all it is just a number that denotes how many times the Earth has rolled around the Sun since the date of our birth. Our age doesn't tell us anything about the difference we have made, or the people we have loved or the struggle we have had to be the person we want to be in this world. It is just a tape measure and it's definitely not an audit report; but yet our age does somehow carry an existential sense of judgement. It places us in a comparative world and ranks us against expectations that we have sometimes imposed on ourselves, and other times have been placed upon us by others.

In 2022, at sixty, the tape measure felt very long, and I found myself wondering what on earth I had achieved. There was nothing on the honours board so to speak, and only a fragile grip of a small business that most people will have never heard of and never will. However, there are stories to tell, and stories that should not be lost.

It was February 2001, and I was walking down Baker Street from Regent's Park. I was early for my meeting so had spent a few minutes wandering around the Park's boating lake, trying not to tread in goose poo, while still taking in the calming view. Now there is a metaphor klaxon if ever there was one! I also remember that I was wearing both a coat and jacket in a vain attempt to be smart and warm, but neither was fitting me very comfortably as a result.

The coffee shop on the corner of Baker Street and Melcombe Street was where I was meeting my client; it was just down the road from the London headquarters Abbey National. Abbey National was the first mutual Building Society to convert to a plc and become a bank. Its reputation was strong, but in a robust muscular way rather than being quietly assured. Abbey was my first client after my decision to leave behind my legal career and to become a consultant; and this was the client meeting to discuss my very first report.

My client contact was Lawrence Smith and there will be much to share about the man called Lawrence later on.

At the time Lawrence worked in the Legal Services Team at Abbey. His role, looking back, was far ahead of its time. Lawrence was a project manager turned head of operations, but not a lawyer. It was then very unusual for a "non-lawyer" to be managing external law firms, project managing significant change programmes for what we would now call their operational model, and generally overseeing the efficiency and effectiveness of the legal team. I had met Lawrence a few times during my project. He was friendly, thoughtful and relentlessly cheerful (attributes I would come to love in the decades that followed) but back then I wasn't sure what he actually did or how he did it. In truth I was a little unsure of the extent of his influence and whether I was being side-lined a little with someone who might know his way around a Gantt chart, but would not really know how a legal team should be organised.

A few months before all of this, I had made the biggest decision of my career. I had been the senior lawyer in not one, but two companies; outwardly I was the success I thought I wanted to be, but in truth I was a little lost and I needed a break from its pressured routines. I needed to find something I wanted to do for myself. I left my role needing to find a different way to be me. I will explore this with you properly in more detail later in the story, but in that Baker Street coffee shop on a chilly February day I want you to know now that at the time I had never felt more vulnerable or less in control of the direction of my life.

Going into the meeting I knew that if Lawrence thought my work was useful and valued I might be able to stick with consultancy for a while longer, but if he didn't like the report and rejected my contribution, I'm not sure I had the courage or the strength to follow this path. Consulting would have become a timid half-embarrassed sentence in an average CV and an episode in my life that would haunt every job interview I would ever have again.

Lawrence had brought a copy of my report with him. It was in Tesco carrier bag, loose leafed with the staple straightened and hanging from one hole on the title page. I could see that he had written notes on every page, but my upside-down reading skills were not up to deciphering his words. As far as I could see there were far too many comments for this to be good news, and my heart sank before he had even started to speak about my work.

I listened to him in that way of someone being dumped from a relationship. I tried not to roll my eyes. I tried not to be so defensive that I looked too fragile to hear the news. But, most of all, I just wanted the conversation to end before the veneer of listening cracked under the pressure of my need to cry.

As Lawrence rummaged for the last page of my report, detached and creased in the plastic carrier bag, he was smiling and his tone was still friendly and positive. I had tuned out from his words, but now I needed to tune back in as our meeting was hopefully about to end.

I remember very clearly what he said. "You know what you are doing, but as you can see this isn't a report I can give my boss written as it is." He went on "The report needs less of your personal opinion and more evidence." And then, "We are not paying you to tell us how things are today, but to help us get to a better place."

Finally, he told me that I needed to answer three questions: The "what?" In other words, what have we got today and why have we got it? Then, the "so what?" Why does it matter and how might it change? And then, the "now what?" The actions needed to make things better.

If I had listened carefully, I would have realised that Lawrence was giving me the most generous, non-patronising and thoughtful masterclass in consulting I could ever wish for, but what I was hearing in that moment was only that "your report is shit and you're fired."

While I was quietly deflating in front of him, Lawrence had something else to say: "So, I have taken all your ideas and put them in the framework I have just explained. I'd like you to read it and be happy with how it now looks, please change anything you don't like. When you are happy, give it back to me with your invoice and I'll make sure you get paid."

He then gave me a copy of my report with his edits. He smiled, rose to his feet, patted me on the shoulder saying, "Thank you Paul, that's great work" and left.

I sat for a few moments with a half-finished cold cappuccino and felt as small and insignificant as anyone could feel. For the next hour or so I stayed in my seat reading the revised report. Part of me hoped I might find fault in it, so I could push back on Lawrence's approach, but the greater part of me was soon overwhelmed with his care, his expertise, his wisdom and his kindness. It was, frankly, a brilliant report, and one that I could never have written at that time.

On that day, Lawrence literally changed the course of my life. It was an example of generous, selfless kindness that I have tried to live up to ever since and one that I will never, ever forget.

A few days later I sent in my revised report. It was accepted in full. My invoice was indeed paid shortly afterwards, and a new career of being a "non-lawyer" was hesitantly, but properly underway. Above all, a priceless and enduring friendship had begun with the most influential soul I have ever met in my life.

I often walk past the coffee shop; it is now a Pret-a-Manger and invariably full of people with laptops, and tourists for the Sherlock Holmes Museum. When I pause on the pavement, I always wonder if anyone else's life has been changed by a conversation in that place. I wonder if we know how the power of kindness can change someone's world not just in the moment, but forever. I wonder if we realise that we have that power too.

02 Give me ten minutes

So now you know a little about Lawrence and a little more about me. There is, of course, much more to say about him, but we will leave Lawrence for now walking back up Baker Street in February 2001 with a tatty old carrier bag that had held the code to my future life in his scribbled notes of insight, care and kindness.

You may already be wondering how this is meant to work as a book, and that would be a fair question. We are only a few pages in, but now is perhaps a good time to set the scene for you, so that you can hopefully relax into the process and read on with a little more anticipation than irritation.

I would like you to think of the stories that are told on these pages as if they are a collection of paintings in a gallery. Some you may like, some not so much; but imagine you are visiting this gallery to see an exhibition that has been put together for you. There is a reason for the exhibition and what has been placed in it, and there is also a reason why you are looking at these pictures.

When Lawrence told me in that coffee shop in 2001 that "We are not paying you to tell us how things are today, but to help us get to a better place," it felt like he had placed a picture in my gallery. For Lawrence this might have been a throw-away line, or perhaps it was something important for him to tell me, but it was certainly important for me to hear it; and it has been a guiding thought for all my work ever since.

The world we occupy, despite all its rush, impatience, deadlines, scurry and hurry, is still speaking to us. Everyday our worlds will offer up to us the wisdom of generations past and present, sharing with us the mistakes which therefore we do not have to make, as well as the gentle moments of inspiration to help us on our way. It is all there for all of us, if only we are open to see, feel and hear what is offered.

In the late nineteen-nineties I was the very busy Head of Legal in a successful financial services business. Cheltenham & Gloucester had been a local building society for a century or more; and for decades it had been quietly efficient and appreciated in a low-key way. Then, under the acquisitive leadership of its Chief Executive Andrew Longhurst, it grew quickly and successfully into a major savings and loan institution of national importance.

I joined the legal team as a one-year qualified lawyer in January 1989 when C&G's upward curve was steep and accelerating. I found the culture to be positive, friendly and supportive; I also felt comfortable in my own skin a way I had not felt before. I was not being judged on my background, my school or where I had trained, but on whether I could help colleagues succeed. There is so much more to say about this, but that story will be for another day and another picture in our gallery.

For now, let's skip forward a few years to my early days as the Head of Legal at C&G, and my first real leadership role. Life was busy and full of meetings, and full of correspondence (yes, I am that old), full of report writing, report giving and… repeat, repeat, repeat. It was typical to have every minute of my day accounted for trying to meet the needs of anyone and everyone who asked for some time. It was not long before grabbing a few diary minutes with me was as hard as if prising apart lift doors stuck fast in a dramatic scene from an action movie.

On such a day, one of my colleagues knocked on my office door and stepped into my room. I was on the phone, but I smiled and gestured that she should come in. I had not seen her for a few days and it would be nice to catch up. She sat in front of me doing that thing when you are not supposed to look at someone on the phone, so she looked out of the window and at the walls and at her notes, all the while being a study of patience. After two minutes of this however we started to conduct

a slightly exaggerated mime of her indicating she would come back later and me indicating that she should stay. No words were exchanged just a lot of knowing eye-brows and hand gestures.

The call ended and I could say hello to her, but that thought had barely time to form the words in my head, when the phone rang again. I could see it was the Chief Executive, so instead of my warm words of greeting I had to say instead "I'm so sorry, it's Andrew, please give me a minute..."

A few minutes later I could at last put the phone down and speak to my colleague. She clearly had something she wanted to tell me and I knew it must be important for her to still be sitting in front of me. Then, just as she started to tell me why she needed a little time, my PA knocked on the door to say that my visitor was waiting and had been waiting for some time already. I felt terrible. I said to my PA that I just needed two more minutes, but my colleague very graciously said that her conversation would wait and that she could see how busy I was. We both made that half-apologising, half-sad face that happens when you know something should be different, but you are not blaming each other.

You might be thinking that this is a fairly non-descript picture to hang in the gallery, but for me it was the moment I realised how precious time really is and how easy it is to use it poorly. I didn't have a diary, my diary had me. Good intentions are not a narrative for making things better, in the end good intentions are just the way we feather our nests of dysfunction to fool ourselves that we will make more time another time, one day, somehow, sometime, soon.

When someone asks if you can give them ten minutes, please truly make it a gift. Let them see that you have made a space solely for them, and in that space listen as if this was the best time and place for only their words to be heard.

Ten minutes can feel like all the time in the world when the calmness of a safe space is shared with kindness and care for the words that will be heard. Ten minutes can also feel like mere moments where carefully crafted ideas are blown away, lost in the teeth of a gale of distractions.

I have put this picture in the gallery not to make an original point, but simply to remind us of something we all know deep down. When we are heard, we feel we belong; when we are not heard, we are lost.

We cannot ever "make time" but we can always try to make time with us feel like a gift worth receiving.

03 United I fell

The next picture I want to show you is less comfortable to write about, but if I am going to ask for your trust as I show you around this exhibition, it is important that you see I have curated this space for you and have not just popped into IKEA for a bit of inspirational wall art.

I left Cheltenham & Gloucester in the summer of 1999. If lawyers were footballers, television pundits would have commented at the time that I was a promising player who had done well so far; industrious rather than creative, a good team member, who was consistent and reliable. The sort of player teams need but for whom the epithet "unsung" was made.

At that time I knew I was neither rounded nor anywhere near the finished article, but I had a fancy job title and I was riding on a wave of corporate success that felt very comfortable to sit on; perhaps too comfortable. I worked hard, but somehow it was easy. C&G was always profitable, always winning and always the darling of the business pages. It was fun, but there came a point when I felt that I was separating from the corporate self-congratulatory messages and the invincibility narrative.

I have learnt a lot about myself in the last twenty-five years and one of the things I can trace back to 1999 is that I do not really trust success. It's quite nice and all that, and who doesn't like praise and a bit of money to go with it, but success doesn't fit me. It's like putting a gold lamé jacket on an anxious introvert.

I don't blame this feeling on anyone else but me, I know it is not altogether healthy, and it is a feeling that sometimes frustrates me a lot, but when things are seemingly going too well I feel like I have been invited to a party where I don't know anyone.

I have come to accept that I am hardwired not to expect to succeed, not to trust it very much when I do, and to feel that the struggle before success is where I properly belong. Ironically, my comfort zone is not very comfortable.

Looking back, and now knowing myself better, it is no surprise that I left C&G when I did. To continue the football metaphor, it was a classy, well coached Premiership team, and I moved to United Assurance who were a relegation threatened Championship team with an illustrious past, but a very uncertain future.

Sadly, United Assurance was united in name only. There were too many new faces brought together at the same time, and it didn't allow for an executive team to build any momentum before market sentiment finally lost patience and dictated that the game was up. United Assurance was sold to Royal London in 2000 and there was I, barely a year into joining them, negotiating my exit.

I know it looks like a major career misstep and it is a very fair interpretation of the bare facts. I left a great job in a great company to take a role in a failing company that hardly lasted twelve months. And yet, I have never regretted my decision to leave C&G nor my decision to move to United Assurance.

I didn't like how success made me feel. It confused me because I knew I had so much more to learn about leading and following and how to make a difference, and yet success was letting me off the hook to learn. Success was the fickle friend who told me that I deserved it, and to fill my boots, but inside I knew I had hardly touched the sides of exploring what I wanted to do and how I wanted to be. I could also see from some of the people around me, that if I truly believed all this was deserved, I was probably one step away from becoming an insufferable arse.

I left C&G when I knew I could grow no more. C&G had been a wonderful opportunity, with wonderful memories and people, and it gave me the platform I needed to properly understand my purpose.

United Assurance however, even though it was messy with incomplete hopes, helped me to see what I needed to know about myself. That said, goodness me, there were some bleak tough times. There were so many days at United when I dreaded going into work; days when I didn't know where to begin and days when nothing made sense, especially me. I felt I had arrived in a remote foreign land not knowing the language, all my luggage containing skills and experience was lost, and I was suffering from a sort of cruel amnesia about how to do my job. It was terribly lonely, but at United I also started to understand some very positive things that have stayed with me forever.

These were the days when I began to realise that being a lawyer might not be my heart song. These were also the days when I started to see that the present moment was more important than anything past or future. In a new role, it didn't matter what I had achieved somewhere else. That story was just a footnote in the new play, not the blockbuster origin story in my blockbuster career franchise. Now is when we make a difference, and we make a difference by being ourselves.

Moving from the outward success of C&G to the outward failure of United, also taught me that you can never judge the quality of people you work with by looking at the share price or by reading the accounts. In a failing company, it is the leaders who have let down the employees, not the employees who have let down their leaders. There are always extraordinary stories in dysfunction, but you must listen and you must care to find them. When people come to work they want to succeed, but if they cannot make their difference, we only lose their contribution to the metrics-du-jour, we do not lose their talent or their kindness, or their passion.

Above all, I learned that there is always a need to do the hard yards of building trust in everything we do. We can never assume that trust will follow even a great idea or a great plan. Trust is the breath that keeps the team's body alive; and it doesn't sit visibly in a business school case study or in a technicolour dream deck of expensive slides.

Today, Lawrence and I often talk about these ideas in our work, but back then I had to figure these things out for myself. If I had known Lawrence then, when I was so lost and often alone, he would have told me that we are all passing through, that nothing is certain, and nothing is permanent. He would have told me that this too will pass, but that listening to colleagues and trying to make them feel just a little bit more comfortable would help me too. Kindness never needs a budget or permission. He would have said that I was doing just fine, and that starting in a new role is harder than anything we ever imagine, and that my confidence was bound to be brittle with so much change in my life. And he would have told me therefore to care a little less about knowing the answer and little bit more about doing what felt right for me in the moment.

United I fell, but I was falling into my future, letting go of things that would otherwise hold me back and holding on to new feelings and new thinking that I hoped would allow me to explore a new way to make my difference.

04 This is how it starts

It nearly always starts with a short, almost inconsequential, text or private message on social media.

"Dear Paul, you don't know me, I am sorry to write to you out of the blue, but I have followed your work for a while, and I wondered if we might be able to have a call. Some things are happening in my work and I would be very grateful for a few minutes of your time."

It may be a short message, but I never underestimate the courage it has taken for someone to ask a complete stranger for help. To have reached this point has probably taken weeks of mulling and stirring about their situation. Then ages spent wondering if they should ask for help, and then pondering who to ask and how to start.

I reflect on this a lot because I know how easy it is for any of us, whatever our privilege, to feel separated from the course we hoped to follow and to feel a little lost. It has nothing to do with status, or position, or competency and skills. It has nothing to do with being strong or weak. Indeed, I know very well how quiet, strong, resilient people may endure dysfunction the longest, but it will still slowly erode them, and it will imperceptibly extract every ounce of coping until there is nothing left for them to give.

In my world I have noticed that those who can tell me what they need are already on their way to a better place; but stubborn, stoic, quiet coping often belies a sense of fading hope and a silent bewilderment of how to help ourselves.

The colleagues who never ask for help, or do not know how to ask, should be the people we look out for the most. I was one of those colleagues once upon a time; unable to put words to my feelings and wondering how I had allowed others to negatively dominate my days so that seemingly non-descript situations would undermine my confidence.

For the most part I have been blessed beyond my imagining in my work, but as I draw to the end of my career and from the perspective of standing on the small hill of my accumulated experience, I can see things that once troubled me terribly, are now just a few pieces in the jigsaw puzzle of my working life. I can also see that these few pieces are surrounded by many more showing the joys, friendships and pride in the picture of my career. Distance doesn't mean we forget the darker days, but it helps us to see them in a different way.

When the new message arrives therefore, asking for my help, I can feel my tummy tumble with the muscle memory of those days when my inexperience infused with anxiety and laced with dread, left me feeling lost and adrift.

We must never, ever, think that someone asking for our help is a chore or an inconvenience. It is a privilege to be the one who is asked to hear what has not been heard and to see what has not been seen. It is the smallest act, to offer a few minutes of our time to someone else, because in that moment we may have offered the first step back into the light.

Leadership starts like this.

I want to make leadership small. Leadership is such an extraordinary word because it often unfurls into something almost mythical. For all of us the word will instantly conjure ideas and personalities well beyond our reality. Ask anyone to name a leader they admire and they might reach for Mandela, Gandhi, Ardern or Zelensky. The temptation is to personify leadership with heroic endeavour and with people who have done amazing things. However, leadership is very rarely about the grand, the powerful or the saintly. It is in the everyday; it is in our every day.

I wrote a blog a few years ago about a time when I visited a client. I wrote about the bombastic General Counsel, John, and the General Counsel's personal assistant, Janet. It was Janet who met me in their office reception.

"Hi Paul, lovely to see you again; John will be with you in just a few minutes, he's on a call, but I'll show you to your meeting room."

We walked along the corridor chatting about Janet's son who was just starting at University and about my daughter's new job. Then, from another meeting room, we heard John abruptly and loudly end his call. He then appeared fully pinstriped in our presence; I was immediately gripped by his overly firm handshake and felt the unspoken signal for no more small talk as I tried to keep up with his exaggeratedly quicker walking pace.

John spoke at me over his shoulder "Paul, I can only give you twenty minutes, I need to be back on another call."

Just before the three of us arrived at our meeting room destination, I noticed a discarded tissue in the corridor. Janet saw it too, bent down and picked it up saying nothing at all. John saw it as well, huffed airily and muttered about the place "going to the dogs".

On my way home that evening I wondered who had been the leader in my day. John had the status, the power and the overly firm handshake to go with his lofty indifference. Janet on the other hand had shown a caring interest in me, enquired and engaged with my needs; and of course she was the person who noticed that something needed to be done and did it.

John may have thought it was beneath him to pick up the tissue, but he was wrong. It was leadership that he failed to grasp, not just a discarded tissue.

Leaders are people who show an authentic thoughtfulness for the people around them, and make their contribution to creating a better place for everyone. When people talk to me about becoming a leader, I will offer this story and ask them if they are not a leader now.

This is how it starts.

If I may stand with you just for a moment. Here we are a little deeper into the exhibition. These pictures are just a few moments in time, like little sketches of events in my life. This is not the whole story, but just a few of the things that have shaped and guided my way. My hope is that you might also reflect on the moments that have become the memories of things that changed the direction of your life.

Please don't keep them in a forgotten corner of your mind, tucked away from your reflection and cares. Bring them out and love the stories they tell you about your past, your today and your tomorrow. Lawrence's Tesco bag once held my future life, and a discarded tissue revealed a lesson in leadership that I will never forget.

As I said at the beginning, we live in times and in places where everything rushes by, but if we always respond by trying to keep up with the giddying swirl, only exhaustion awaits us. If we allow ourselves to pause and to notice, then it is possible that we may see how everything speaks to us and how everything reacts with us. If we then share what has touched us, we give permission for others to pause and to share too.

I am certain that leadership does not start with a grand plan and a grander sense of self. Leadership starts when we notice the quiet ones and listen. It starts when we see what small differences we can make and then act on what we have seen. Leadership starts when there is no plan and little sense of self. It starts when we stand with people and care about the pictures they would like to bring out and share.

This is how it starts. Leadership, not as a management theory, but as a story of moments of reflection and change. Moments we notice and then hold close to our hearts to help us make sense of the paths we have taken; but also to help others tell their stories too.

Leadership is small, so even when we reach for the smallest pebble of kindness, and when it is cast with care, we will create ripples of hope that move far beyond our sight. This is how it starts.

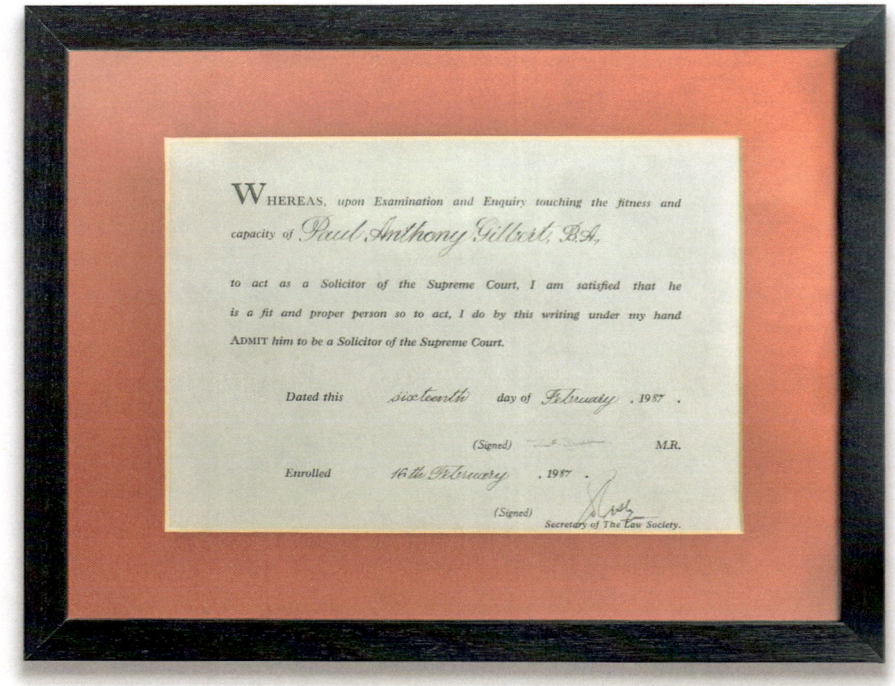

05   We are all passing through

An exhibition should be more than just a series of pleasant pictures that say the same or similar things. An exhibition should carry us into a story so that we may see something more clearly, or to challenge our settled thoughts. An exhibition should be a story that unfolds as we walk from room to room, and which encourages us to take with us the impressions, ideas and the truth of what we have found. An exhibition is both the moments we spend in front of each picture and the memories that the pictures ask us to hold when we leave.

I have often said that the proudest day of my professional life was 16 February 1987. It was on this day that I became a solicitor in the jurisdiction of England and Wales. A date I am reminded of almost every day because of a small, unprepossessing and now age-faded certificate that is framed quietly in the corner of my office. The certificate is headed "In the Supreme Court" and it goes on to state, rather grandly, that:

"Whereas, upon Examination and Enquiry touching the fitness and capacity of Paul Anthony Gilbert to act as a Solicitor of the Supreme Court, I am satisfied that he is a fit and proper person so to act."

The certificate is signed by the Master of the Rolls who at the time was Sir John Donaldson. By his elegant, elderly, hand this Law Lord of the Supreme Court, admitted me to the legal profession and into a life that just a few years before was beyond my imagining.

This piece of paper does not define me, but it signifies something almost existential about my life. The date marks the moment in time when my life changed in a far more profound way than any mere qualification date might otherwise suggest.

In the span of a working life, our first job is typically a stepping-stone to something bigger and which points in a direction that suggests greater things. In a world where we might need to pass an exam to be allowed to do our job, the qualification date is the starting gun not the medal ceremony.

Therefore, back then in February 1987, aged twenty-four and eleven months, to most observers I would have been just one more young person standing in the foothills of his career. Ahead of me men and women of great reputations and fabulous achievements, would be able to point to a whole mountain range of opportunities with their snow-capped peaks of likely achievement to come. I was just starting out with everything in front of me. Back then, I knew so little and could be rightly and easily ignored. No-one knew me at all, I had done nothing. And yet, I knew so, so clearly that this date of admission was no foothill; I knew it was already the biggest mountain I would ever have to climb. Whatever else I might do, whatever paths I might take, I would never climb anything this high ever again.

This was not a stepping-stone or a starting gun for me, this was when I stood up, put my future in my pocket, and walked into the world. I was now released from the expectations of my past and given the miracle of countless future possibilities to explore.

Looking back on the span of thirty-six years since that day in 1987, I do not judge myself as to whether I made good or bad choices. I do not wonder "what if?", or regret what might have been; but I do feel blessed that I could choose. For many people I work with, making the right decision, especially about their careers, is all important and all consuming. It preoccupies their thinking before, during and after the decision is made. I firmly believe however, that all our decisions, especially about the roles we take, matter far less than the opportunity every new role gives us to explore, learn and grow.

It does not matter where we are, it only matters that it helps us to tell our story.

As I guide you through this exhibition, and show you the pictures I have placed here for you, it is also the case that each new role you take will offer you time to stand within it as a picture in your career. Then, when you leave, you will take the memories of each role with you, holding them with care.

At the start of my working life, and now in my sixties, I know that nothing has ever mattered to me more than to honour the freedom that I was given on 16 February 1987 to make decisions about the roles I wanted to explore.

I have shown you my admission certificate and told you how it matters so much to me, but it was nearly thirty years later that my dearest friend, Lawrence, captured a thought so beautifully about the freedom to make decisions that it is also now a picture I would like to share with you in this exhibition.

We were sitting in a hotel bar on the banks of the River Cam. The late summer sun was setting, and we had just completed an especially tiring and stressful assignment with a difficult client. Weeks of work and two days of presentations were now over. We both knew it had been a miserable time and no amount of money we might invoice would ever truly compensate for the feeling of having been used for an agenda that was not shared with us at the time. We decided in that moment never to put ourselves in this position again and we changed the direction of our business that evening with the clink of our beer glasses and a handful of dry-roasted peanuts.

I love Lawrence so much; from tatty Tesco carrier bag to now, he has been my guiding North Star. He cares so much to do the right thing, and will never let anyone down, yet he also holds tension and pressure so lightly and lets bad things gently drift away. Here we were, fed-up and a bit bruised, but Lawrence lent back in his chair, smiled and gestured that we should have another drink; as he got up to walk to the bar, he gently tapped my shoulder and said, "Hey, you know what, no matter what, we're all just passing through Paul, we're all just passing through".

A working life is a kind of miracle. Over time we have the good fortune to collect memories and experiences that help us to make sense of our past, which help us to grow in the moment, and which shift countless possible futures into our line of sight for us to contemplate and consider. Not everything will be joyful, sometimes our plans and hopes will be confounded, and sometimes we will be hurt, but like beachcombers on the shoreline of the roles and opportunities we are blessed to pass by, there is always something to collect along the way and our talent is always, now and forever, our permission to roam.

06 How Ian McKellen and Linda Loman changed my life

This next part of the exhibition will take a bit of explanation and introduction, and I need to take you into a different room. This is going to be less of an exhibition space and much more of a performance space. I want it to be a place that is comfortable, but one which also lets you hold up your talent for others to help you explore.

In a funny sort of a way it starts in 1978 and a school trip to the Merlin Theatre in Frome, Somerset.

I was at school at Kingdown Comprehensive in Warminster, a small army garrison town equidistant between Bath and Salisbury on the A36. As part of my English Literature O-Level I was reading Twelfth Night. That year a touring production of the play had arrived just down the road in Frome. In this production a 39-year-old Ian McKellen was Malvolio and the theatre company was running what we would call today a "schools out-reach programme", but I suspect back then I might have called it a cheeky skive day. On this day however, it was my school's turn to have a workshop with the actors in the morning and to then watch the play performed in the afternoon.

For all my life I have felt that theatres are magical places where disbelief is suspended and joy, insight, tears and truth are built from words that have been handed down as a gift for us to reflect on and relish. I suspect this feeling goes back to 1978 and this day in Frome.

As we filed into the theatre for the workshop, the auditorium was empty, still and dark; every plush red velvet seat arcing around the stage in comfortable expectation. In contrast, the stage was brightly lit in a pure, almost dazzling, white light. The stage was austerely empty save for three white stage flats and one white door frame, but without its door.

I was immediately intrigued, excited and nervous. I had been expecting something a lot more, well, theatrical with extravagantly painted scenery, exotic furniture and props a plenty; but here in this empty nothingness how would a complex play unfold with barely a clue as to how anything might be told?

Of course, 1978 is a long time ago and I don't have a perfect memory about the day, but I do remember something very clearly and it has stayed with me preciously ever since. My class was invited to sit on the stage with Ian McKellen and he asked us to work in pairs. He wanted us to hold the head of our partner to see how heavy a head can feel. He said it was an exercise in trust, because to feel how heavy a head really is, the neck has to be so relaxed as to let the head be held without any of the neck's help.

As it happened there were an odd number of children in the class and I was the one left behind without a partner. Ian asked me to join him and be his partner for the exercise. He first asked me to hold his head and I was astonished how heavy it was. I felt like I was holding a hairy medicine ball and I needed to brace myself not to show I wasn't that strong. Then it was my turn, and I couldn't do it; I couldn't relax my neck muscles to let Ian hold my head. I remember him quietly and gently admonishing me for not trusting him as I nervously and inadvertently tensed my neck again. We chatted for a few seconds and then he said, "I won't drop it you know and let it roll off the stage." I laughed and he held my head again. This time I did it, and I felt what it was like to trust someone else for a few seconds and how energising and reassuring that could be.

I knew it was an important moment, but I just didn't know why or how. This would only reveal itself to me much, much later in my life.

That afternoon we watched Twelfth Night. It is such a silly play really and while I remember it fondly, I don't want to rush to see it now. I guess that to my adolescent mind I didn't really get past the slapstick moments and I certainly don't think I ever really got the layers of psychological drama. However, I do remember one thing so clearly about the performance. I remember how transfixed I was by how the actors could occupy a white empty space with just a single white door frame and make me feel that I was in a real world, with real things happening all around me. I know I will never forget that sense of how they were able to create space, light, shapes and feelings by the way they were with each other and with their audience.

It would be trite to extrapolate from that afternoon and say I found a truth that guided my later work ambitions. That didn't happen. Back then I am pretty certain I had a typical teenager's attention span, a need for chips and no significant space for serious deep thinking; but something happened that day for sure. A spark, or a small thought, that was then and is still today very precious and very real.

When Lawrence and I sat down in 2006 to create our first training event we didn't start with an agenda about content or even themes; we started with just one question – how do we want people to feel?

Training is about helping people to be more familiar and more comfortable, and ultimately more expert in the tasks they need to perform. It is about passing on knowledge and skills in policy, process and techniques and it is therefore an essential and important part of working life. It's just not what I have ever wanted to do. The ambition that Lawrence and I shared in 2006 was not to train anyone in anything.

When I watched Ian McKellen on stage, with just white light and a door frame for company, he created a world with words and with suggestion that was just as real as if I had been washed up on the shores of Illyria myself. He didn't train me to feel like this, he didn't instruct me to reveal certain emotions at certain times, but he created a space and gave me the opportunity to be more of myself than I had ever felt before.

death of a Salesman

At the time I was just a boy and I can assure you I was not piecing all of this together and making notes for my future career (to be honest, I wouldn't have known then what the word "career" meant anyway). And I certainly did not rush home that evening to tell mum and dad that I'd had a bit of a moment and it might shape my thinking for the rest of my life. However, something very important had lodged in my heart that day and it has never left me since.

A few months on from this day in a small theatre in Frome, with Twelfth Night now being revised so hard that I can still quote from it today, I had another theatre experience that was even more profound. This time it helped me to see something so precious that I am worried I won't have the words to tell you about it in the way I would like you to feel it too.

It was another school trip, this time to Bath, to see a performance of Death of a Salesman with Warren Mitchell as Willy Loman. Please remember, I am just a teenage boy doing my O Levels. I have not yet kissed a girl and I am far too shy to notice if anyone might want to kiss me; although, to put it another way, I am totally convinced that no one in their right mind will ever want to kiss me. I am six foot tall, but thin as a rake, and I have a perennial spot on the side of my nose that makes me feel like I'm attached to a cartoon car horn. I don't do conversation because I don't feel I have anything to say. I dress not to be noticed and I worry that I do not have opinions on anything. I can't quote Monty Python sketches word for word and I can't get into the heavy metal music that my classmates bang on about all the time. Instead, I quite like ABBA and so this becomes something else that I cannot say out loud. If I could just quietly watch a Test Match on TV from first ball to last, that would be my happy place. This is my introvert world where I have hardly read a book that I was not asked to read by a teacher, where I have never been on a plane and where London feels like a place that only really exists in films and on TV.

It was this boy who went to see a play about a middle aged-man losing his job, watching his family fall apart and then he dies. However, the boy who left the theatre that night, who had cried and cried through the pain, and the love, and the dignity, and the shame, and the honesty, and the hopeless relentless pressure of poverty, and the hope of providing a better life, and the hope of redemption, and the power of enduring love; well, that boy was different and he would never, ever, be the same again.

I have been to every UK production of this play ever since. The last time was with Wendell Pierce as Willy Loman and Sharon D Clarke as his wife Linda. I cried again, of course I did, I cried for the boys, for Willy, for Linda, for their struggle and their fate. I cried for her indomitable love, pride and dignity. I cried for Willy's weakness and loss of self. I cried for the pain an indifferent world can create, and I cried because all that was needed was for the world to show them just a little more understanding, love and kindness, and to respect the dignity of one inconsequential family's suffering.

As a teenage boy walking away from the theatre in Bath, with no discernible direction of travel for his young life, I realised a few things that I had not quite realised before. I now knew deep in my bones that everyone counts and that everyone struggles. I knew that no one is free of pain and that most people can hide their pain really well. Life is hard. Good people screw up sometimes. And love, real unconditional, selfless love, can hurt like hell, but without it we are lost.

I also knew that beautifully written words can change lives. Arthur Miller's words changed mine. Beautiful words that create such powerful feelings will also connect us to our own sense of self, of belonging and of needing to be ourselves. I owe Ian McKellen a great deal, but I owe most to Linda Loman.

When Lawrence and I sat down together in 2006 to write the first LBCambridge programme, we were never ever going to create a training event. We only ever wanted to make people feel something that would be just for them, not for their bosses or for their organisations, but for them. We wanted to help them feel that they had not even begun to understand the shape of their potential and to start believing in their power to explore it.

In 2006, like my teenage self, our first event was awkward and shy, but as the years have rolled by we are more certain than ever that our purpose is not to train, but to connect people to their potential, to help them grow and to make their difference.

If you will allow me therefore, please let me hold your hand in this performance space in our exhibition, where there are no pictures to show you, just the white light of a small theatre in Somerset in 1978. If you feel that you can gently and safely reveal a little of your soul, as Ian McKellen and Linda Loman encouraged me to reveal a little of mine, I believe you will find a feeling of certainty and truth, of love and trust, that will stay with you forever.

May I also share with you this thought, that how we make people feel is something we should notice. How we want people to feel is something we should influence with care and kindness. And knowing how people would like to feel around us, is a gift from them to us that we should treasure and hope that we can fulfil.

07 The Yellow House

We have moved through a few of the exhibition rooms and settled for a while in the performance space, but it is time now to move somewhere else where we can pause to take an even more reflective look at our story.

From the bright white light of the Merlin Theatre stage in 1978, I want to take you into a small room in 1990 which, in contrast, is very dimly lit indeed. The light is soft, almost velvety, and seems to be a deep, dark blue. It definitely isn't black, or cold, or unwelcoming; so even though it is dark, this feels like a place where we can rest our whirligig minds and be safe with our quietest thoughts.

In the summer of 1990, I was in Amsterdam holding a ticket to enter the van Gogh centenary exhibition at the van Gogh Museum. Looking back, I'm not sure why I first became quite so fascinated by Vincent's story; perhaps it was because he was the man who never sold a painting in his life, but who was revered as a genius after his death. Maybe it was his obvious vulnerability and vivid pain; or maybe it was just that the swirling skies and fireworks of colour in his work spoke to my own swirling thoughts and a mind of tumbling colours. Whatever it was, I loved his work.

However, until this day in 1990 I had never seen a painting by van Gogh in real life. The centenary exhibition was the biggest collection of his work anywhere, ever, with paintings and drawings loaned from private collections and museums from all over the world; and I had a ticket.

I was near the front of the queue at the main entrance to the Museum, and when the doors opened at 10am, I was quickly inside and standing in a large open foyer between galleries of his work. I remember feeling a little overwhelmed and I wasn't sure what to do or where to go. This was partly my unfamiliarity with how places like this work, but mostly it was because the museum was filling up very quickly with hundreds of people pouring through the doors. For a few moments I had become a slightly bewildered and gently jostled Brit, and it was not quite the contemplative experience I had been hoping for. I decided to get ahead of the shuffling crowds and so I walked as briskly as I could through Vincent's early life story, not pausing to look at anything, and then up three or four flights of stairs, until I arrived in a small quiet room well above the entrance hall and the milling throng of visitors below. I had walked past probably two-thirds of the exhibition, but now at least I was on my own.

As I entered the room, my eyes had to adjust to the dark blue velvety light. It wasn't too dark to see, but it was a good few seconds before I could feel orientated in the space. In the centre of the room was a single painting. I didn't recognise the picture and I couldn't recall seeing it before in any book or magazine. It was called "The Yellow House". I was still the only person in the room, and it was so peaceful and so calm; it was as if the dark blue velvety light was absorbing all sounds. The painting was illuminated by a single spotlight, but I swear when I first saw it, it was the picture that was shining its light from the canvass, like pouring light through a window.

At that moment, in that place, I felt like I was with him. I felt like we were standing there together just looking at his painting. I could see his layers of paint like the ripples made by receding waves over wet sand. I could see the rough edges and the scrapes. I could see the depth of colour as if the paint itself was a landscape; and I could see how boldly and beautifully the colours threw off their light. It felt like I was being shown someone's diary, like they were telling me things that were deeply precious to them. I felt included and involved. It also looked for all the world, like he had only just finished the painting; like he might have popped out to wash his hands. It seemed to me as if the paint could still be moved around the canvass, soft, yielding and not yet dry. I felt like I was the first person to see it.

I was fixed in front of it, unable and unwilling to move. I stood and stared in a profound silence, aware of tears on my face. I wasn't crying (for a change) I was just moved to my core by something so crushingly beautiful, so raw, so human and yet so apparently ordinary too. After all, it was just an ordinary yellow house on the corner of an ordinary street.

I think I knew then, seeing the Yellow House for the first time, that there could never be anything ordinary in this world, and that all around us there would be people with their stories that should be seen and heard. As I look back on that day, with three more decades of accumulated experience, I cannot say for sure I knew then how important it would become for me to help others to find their stories, but I can say that this is where it began. It feels part of me now, and whenever I find myself in Amsterdam, I always pay a visit to see the Yellow House and it always takes my breath away.

At this point, I do not want to sound like some happy-clappy evangelist asking you to step onboard the cliché tram and play mindfulness bingo with me, but I do want to take you to that room in Amsterdam in 1990. If you were there with me and saw what I saw, and felt what I felt, you would also believe that there are stories all around us, in all of us and in everything. But first we must notice them, then we must allow the stories to speak to us and then we must let the stories stay with us.

The first and most important story is our own. The reflective pause I would like you to make therefore, is not some momentary distraction from your busy day; the pause I want you to make is to create a stillness in your life for your own story to catch up with your swirling, spinning world. The very best person to tell your story is you; and my worry is that in all the hectic to and fro, you haven't even noticed it.

This is easy to say, I know. We pack our lives with lists, rushing from one responsibility to another. We fill our time with duty and let the world scrape at our soul. Reflection feels like indulgence and a pause just means we fall further behind; and anyway who else is going to change the bed, shop for food, write that report, have that

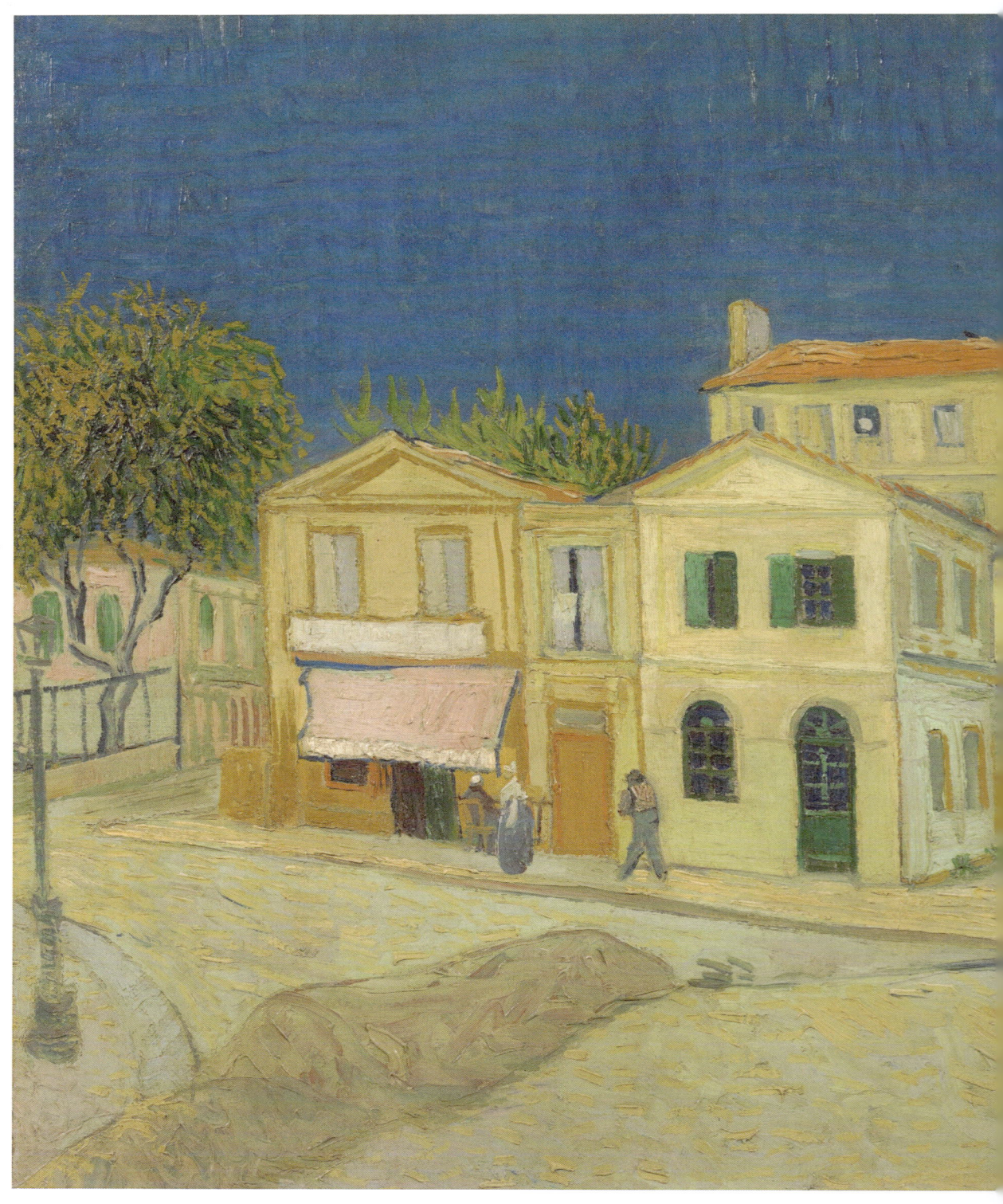

'The Yellow House'
Van Gogh Museum, Amsterdam
(Vincent van Gogh Foundation)

meeting that doesn't matter and also remember it is someone's birthday so their card must be posted tomorrow?

However, this is a beautiful story too. It may not be the story you dreamed of, but it is still a beautiful story. We need to know our own story, or else we are flotsam, accidentally thrown overboard into the currents of other peoples' unthinking ways. Reflection is not an indulgence, it is how we navigate our past so that we can be present in our today. A pause does not mean we fall behind, it means we do not travel too far in a direction we did not intend, or that we can push forward knowing the path we are on is just right for us, for now.

When we know our own story, the more we will know how to make our difference. When we know our own story the more we can help others to make their difference too. Mentoring is then the realisation that when we notice and when we listen, the stories that were hiding in plain sight become real and valuable for the people who are now noticed and heard, and also for us too.

To mentor is not to give advice, or to judge or challenge. It is only ever to make the space for someone else to find their story in their own words. On one summer's day in 1990, in a dimly lit room in Amsterdam, I discovered something about myself and something about the world I lived in. It was the start of realising that there was even more to notice than I had thought.

In the end, it was not the picture of an ordinary yellow house that moved me, but the man who left his heart and soul for me to discover in the marks he made on a canvass a century before. In this moment of discovery, it was not about the art, but about Vincent finding his way to talk to me; and all I had to do was be kind enough to notice and to listen.

All any of us have to do is be kind enough to notice and to listen.

08 From Badlands to bright lights

Earlier in this exhibition I showed you the story of leaving Cheltenham & Gloucester and moving to United Assurance, but how I got to C&G is the next picture I want to show you, because the things we learn at the beginning stay with us the longest, and we rely on them the most.

In January 1989, eighteen months before I was visiting the van Gogh Museum and discovering the Yellow House, I moved from a small general practice law firm at the foot of the Malvern Hills in Worcestershire, to the legal team of a major high street financial institution with three-hundred branches across the UK, known then as the Cheltenham & Gloucester Building Society.

For most of the previous year and having only just qualified, I had not been thinking about leaving, but I knew I didn't feel settled either. I was making friends and starting to find my way, but I also felt detached from the world I was in. I didn't know how to be me, and I wasn't sure if being perpetually grateful for my opportunity was going to be enough to sustain me if the same opportunity was also making me feel unhappy.

Then one day I was flicking through the Law Society Gazette and I saw an advertisement for a junior consumer credit lawyer in C&G's legal team. Until that moment I had never contemplated becoming an in-house lawyer and it had never been part of any conversation that I can recall. To be honest, I am still unsure why this role appealed to me, I didn't even have my own credit card.

I wish I still had my CV from that time – what could I possibly have said? My typical week included drunk and disorderly bail applications, County Court advocacy, crushingly sad divorce cases and the occasional trips to Gloucester Prison to take defendant statements.

Memory plays tricks, but when I think back to how it was for me then, I have a strong sense of needing to move on, of feeling closed-in and that this was not the place for me to stay. However I do not want to pretend there was a plan. Hindsight is brilliant at extracting a compelling narrative from scrambled thinking, but there was no plan. That said, I have always known that when dark clouds gather in my life it is important for me to find some light and to move towards it. I definitely needed to find some light, and may be that is why I found the advertisement compelling.

The way I would describe this today is that we are never totally captured by circumstances that make us sad if we can still describe a future where we can be more of our true selves and where we can shine again. However, I don't want to sound ungrateful for my time in Malvern; while I was unhappy, I also know that without my training contract and without the one chance I had been given to start my career as a lawyer, nothing I have done since would have been possible.

There are other things I am grateful for too. In the relatively short time I was there I learnt so much about people, about listening and being present for those who are sad, worried and confused. Hardly anyone walked through the front door of the office because they wanted to, most people were traumatised, broken or breaking. I was in my twenties without an ounce of real-life to back up my words, but I held their hopes with all the care that I could. Most people who have problems are lonely with them, ensuring that they were heard was the least I could do.

When I found the Yellow House in Amsterdam, I understood how everyone's story mattered and should be told. I saw how extraordinary we all can be. But, working in Malvern at this time I didn't have the vocabulary to make people feel valued. All I could do was listen and care, and I wasn't sure it was enough.

I also learnt how unattractive entitlement can seem and how little respect some people have for other people's points of views and other people's lives. I realised that I wasn't cut out for aggressive letter writing or being the mouth-piece for bullies. I wasn't streetwise, I wasn't artful and I may have watched too many episodes of Petrocelli for my own good, but I wasn't going to be anyone's hired help to make other people unhappy.

The partners who offered me my place in this extraordinary profession, gave me the chance of a lifetime to start my career, and while I found it hard, uncomfortable and sometimes an ordeal, I will always look back on that gift with humility and gratitude. I posted my CV to C&G with about as much hope as if it had been rolled up inside a bottle and gently dropped into the sea off the end of a pier. This was not part of a thought through career plan, and as the daily churn of jobs and tasks gripped me again, I promptly forgot all about it.

Then one day, weeks later, I took a call from a stranger who would not tell our office receptionist who she was. It was C&G's Chief Solicitor's secretary asking me if I might be interested in going for an interview.

I had never been in large corporate building before. It was HUGE. So much bustle, with open-plan lines of desks and ringing phones; lanyards, vending machines, sofas, pop-up banners and a sort of friendly anonymity, and it all appealed so much. There seemed to be so many people in animated conversation, walking briskly to and fro, stepping in and out of lifts, speaking fast and knowingly, and it was all wonderfully intoxicating. I could not begin to imagine what they all did, but it felt sophisticated and important. It was like a campus for grown-ups where people seemed to be enjoying their days and where you couldn't imagine hearing the sound of sobbing, or violent teenagers kicking doors.

The interview seemed to go ok, but I remember being told that my lack of any consumer credit experience was not ideal. Inevitably, a few days later, a letter duly arrived thanking me for my interest, but declining to take my application further.

I wasn't really that disappointed; I wouldn't have employed me either, but it was nice to have glimpsed a totally different world, and I knew then that whatever happened, my future would be somewhere else.

I settled back into a world of anxious bail applications and Green Form advice for sad souls. But something else had happened to me at this time as well. For the first time I saw that to be this type of lawyer, and to do it well, was an extraordinary and important vocation. C&G's corporate headquarters was intoxicating for sure, and it really did feel important, but I also knew that nothing should ever be more important than fighting for someone's liberty, or keeping children secure in a broken family, or helping the wife of a bastard husband find her way to safety and a future without violence.

I realised that I could do this type of work, and in time I felt I would learn to do it really well. I knew how vital it was that that good people should want to do this work, but I also knew it would take a toll on me. In this place, at this time, was not where I belonged. It was time to leave.

About a month after my interview and with my letter of rejection long forgotten, I had another call from C&G, this time inviting me back for a second interview. The only candidate with a nodding acquaintance with the right bit of legislation had decided not to move from their current employer. The process was back on, and I was still in the game. My second interview seemed to turn on one question, "So, Paul, would you be prepared to learn about the Consumer Credit Act?" Given that earlier in the week my only suit was being dry-cleaned after I had slipped in a field trying to serve an injunction on a builder with a nasty temper; the question was not too difficult to answer. And so it was that three months later I moved from the badlands of Barnards Green in Malvern, to the bright lights of an in-house lawyer's life in Cheltenham.

From the distance of my great age today and the decades that have passed, I know it was not Wall Street or the Square Mile, but this was by far the biggest possible change I could ever imagine in my working life. Of course, I had no idea if I could do the job, but I knew in my bones that I was stepping into a world where I could be more of myself than I had dared to be before, and where I could therefore grow and where I could make my difference. It felt liberating and energising, and I felt lucky as hell.

'Sacred Heart' by Jeff Koons

09 Giving it up

We are making great progress through the exhibition and there are just a few more pictures to show you. There will be some very precious things to share, but first I need to reflect with you on a darker time. When the light dims, and it will for all of us at some time, whatever we may feel we have become we are never less than we were before. Then, when the light returns, and it will, we will make our difference again, but this time with a depth of insight and understanding about being human that surpasses whatever we have understood before.

It is the year 2000, and my role at United Assurance is now sadly over. The business could not be revived and has now been sold to Royal London, and I have left the office for the last time having said my goodbyes to a team I had begun to love, but from whom I had not had a chance to learn as much as I hoped.

It was not an overly emotional time to be honest, and there was quite a lot of relief in walking away from what has been a difficult role to fill. With events turning so fast, there was no time to make a lasting difference and no achievement to call my own. I was walking away from a relentless and overwhelming feeling of being part of a giant fire-fighting Whack-A-Mole theme park. The abiding feeling on my last drive home was of exhaustion, not of sadness or loss.

Exhaustion, however, I discovered can be a corrosive state. I was still only 38 years old and had just finished my second General Counsel role. I had also been Chair of the Law Society Commerce & Industry Group and had become a member of the Law Society's governing Council. I think friends and former colleagues expected me to quickly find a new General Counsel adventure, moving on in leaps and bounds through my ever upwards and onwards career journey. We all know however that what we believe about ourselves and hide inside, can be vastly different to what others believe they see on the outside. My bathroom mirror observed me more closely than anything else, and it would have told a very different story.

For most mornings after I had left United, for what seemed like weeks on end, I would look in that mirror each morning to shave and my darkened, tired eyes would fill with quiet tears. I was a bit lost.

How I felt is hard to describe, but I was empty, and at this time I didn't want to be a General Counsel anymore. My inner critic, after years of moulding, had finally crafted the perfect imposter. On the outside I was plausible, likeable and successful, but on the inside I was hollowed out by self-doubt and now I was almost ashamed to even apply for new roles, so unconvinced I was of my credentials. It was like living a real-life anxiety dream, but instead of waking from the nightmare into a plausible reality, this one followed me around even when I wasn't asleep. I had been found out and I couldn't see anyone wanting to employ me ever again.

When exhaustion is like this, it is an acid that seeps into every vulnerability, and it left me feeling weakened and in pain. Nothing had prepared me for believing that my career as a lawyer might be over and I didn't have the words to use to ask for help or to seek reassurance. So, I said nothing to anyone, not even my family. It might pass after all, and then I would look even more foolish than I already felt.

Looking back, I now know what was happening to me. I know the patterns and the shapes and the feelings, and it doesn't scare me like it did back then. My exhaustion had become a mental health concern.

In the space of eighteen months, I had left the security and familiarity of C&G where I knew the people, the politics, the hidden pathways and how to make it work; and now at United Assurance I had to ask how to use the staff canteen, and claim expenses, and everyone's name at least three times. I was commuting from Gloucestershire to the North West, living out of overnight bags and on takeaway food, while disrupting family life and being dislocated from friends and that precious feeling of simply belonging. Then I found that my new company was failing fast, and so I continued to commute because there was no point in relocating. Soon I was involved in the sale of United, the biggest deal I had ever done, and I was struggling to be useful for my Board and to the wider business that was an employer of thousands of people all of whom were now anxious for their own uncertain futures. Everyone it seemed was sad and fed up and unable to be their best, but the deal still had to be done.

And then suddenly it was over, and I drove away with a box of personal papers in the boot of my car.

I was not just exhausted, I was almost certainly depressed. I had a low mood, a loss of confidence, a sense of things closing in and I wanted to hide away even from those who loved me. However, in 2000 I didn't know that this was depression and I didn't go to my doctor. In my head, this was my fault and it was mine to endure. In my head I was simply a self-diagnosed failure and the punishment was to be me.

While I was profoundly sad, weakened and alone, I have never regretted this time. It was a gift that opened my eyes to how we are all capable of being amazing and at the same time being crushingly vulnerable as well. It was a gift that changed my life. We must not hide that which might undermine us; but accept that our vulnerability is part of our story, and it is what makes our success so much more precious and real. We are not avatars. Our stories are kaleidoscopes of experiences and feelings and far richer that anyone knows; and when our stories are shared the world around us shines in colours and opportunities we had never appreciated before.

What followed for me, now holding this gift as tightly as I could, was an opportunity I would never have thought possible for someone like me, and it became the greatest adventure of my life. The darkness was indeed just before the dawn.

10 Now what?

The Golden Heart in Nettleton Bottom holds a special place in this story and in this exhibition. It was where I met Geoff Williams on a cool summer's evening having left United Assurance a couple of months before. It is still 2000 and I have a decision to make about my career and about who I am.

Geoff was the Company Secretary at C&G when I was there. He joined not long after me, hand-picked by our Chief Executive. He was a little intimidating to meet at first, immaculately dressed, quite formal in tone, and unashamedly precise in language both written and spoken.

Despite my casual and often eccentric acquaintance with English grammar rules, we became great friends. Geoff was not a lawyer, but I think I learned more from him about how to be a lawyer than anyone else in my life. He is the cleverest person I have ever met, with strong views and wide, eclectic interests. He is fearless in pursuing what is right and defiant in the face of bullshit. He is politically astute, but never, ever has he played politics.

I have always described Geoff as my mentor. He is a man of wisdom and compassion who is meticulous in his work, but generous and supportive at the same time. His standards are almost impossibly high, but you will never feel inadequate in his presence. He embodies the word "professional" and I aspired to carry just some of his gravitas and assurance. He is someone I love very much and whose opinion I have always sought on all my most important decisions.

The Golden Heart is a faded, unpretentious sixteenth century pub with flagstone floors, nooks, alcoves and ceilings designed to catch out first-time visitors. Nettleton Bottom nestles in a dip between Cheltenham and Cirencester and is a place that could not be further removed from corporate life or my existential career anxieties.

We met so that I could talk to him about something I was struggling to share with anyone else. I wanted to tell him that I was unsure if I would ever apply for a new General Counsel role again; I wanted to tell him that I was struggling and lost.

In the end I couldn't bring myself to talk about the pain I felt, but looking back I have the strongest feeling that I didn't need to. And it makes me love him even more.

I told Geoff that I wanted to help lawyers be more effective, to feel more valued and to find a way to enjoy their roles more. I wanted our contribution to be more than advisory, but vital and right. I wanted us to look after each other, but to know we carried a responsibility for interests wider than the narrow priorities of a pressing task list. I wanted us to speak up when others wouldn't or couldn't, I wanted us to be proud of the difference we made, of the harm we prevented and the good we achieved.

I was enthusiastic and positive, but my ideas lacked any of the detail I knew that Geoff would typically seek. I half expected him to tell me I was a bloody fool; that I was at the height of my powers and it was madness to start something new that no-one had told me was needed. And that I was forgoing salary and security and potentially trashing my CV for an inconsequential diversion.

I pressed on, and Geoff listened quietly without pushing back on anything I said. I told him that I knew people struggled, that it was a lonely place sometimes, but that there were things we could all do better and that I believed people would pay for help and guidance they could trust. I guess you don't have to be a psychotherapist to know that I was describing my pain, and that the idea to help others was in part a projection of that pain, and in part a hope that I would find a way to help myself.

Geoff told me he was proud of me. I still hold those few words close to my heart even now. He said I had a chance to do something different and important, and that he trusted my judgment that this would work. I heard his words and it felt like I was being released from a trap.

We talked and talked and, as we did so in this quiet corner of Gloucestershire calm, I could feel that I was turning a corner and the light might not be dimmed forever.

The relief I felt was huge. I think I needed permission not to conform, but I needed to hear this from Geoff whose judgement was always unswerving and true. All my life I had tried to fit in and never really succeeded, but now for a while at least I could try to find my own way. Geoff gave me that permission and I will always be indebted to him for his love and care at that time.

The truth of the matter, of course, was that in so many ways this was a bloody foolish idea. I had no plan, no clue, no clients, no one to follow, no model to repeat. Geoff would have known this too, but he didn't say a word against it. I think he knew, as I did, that in this dark place, we couldn't extinguish any light I might be holding, however flickering and small it might be.

The wisest man I knew had given me permission to gently hold a very unwise idea. For every single one of us there are going to be times when we need to hold an unwise idea and still be told we are loved and that people are proud of us. Sometimes, doing the right thing for us means to necessarily separate ourselves from the crowd. Sometimes doing the right thing for others is to support them when they need to do this too.

Even as I write these words and see them on the page for the first time, I am deeply moved by how kind and profound his encouragement was for me. I felt heard and I felt understood. I felt it might be ok to be me.

This was going to be my way back. I would meet, listen to, and help as many lawyers as possible. I would share what I found. I would claim no insight that was special to me, nor credit for the ideas I shared, but I would share and keep sharing. The more people I could meet, the more ideas I would be able to share. I was not wise myself, nor did I want to be a self-appointed guru, or claim to be an expert in anything; I was just going to be me, meeting good people, listening to them and sharing whatever I could.

However, at no point did I feel that this would be my forever path. More than anything, I just needed to take some control of my vulnerability, and I needed to find a way to pause the relentlessness of how careers are so often perceived. I also needed to learn my craft. There is still no required training to prepare you for becoming a General Counsel; back then I had already had two such roles and in different ways I was ill-equipped for both. I was determined that this must never happen to me again.

The next few months, perhaps for the next year or more, I was going to learn from everyone I met. Then, when I might apply for my next General Counsel role, whenever that might be, I was going to be a fucking awesome candidate. I would carry the wisdom and experiences with me of the very best people in the legal profession. I would know the importance of the role and how to use its power well. I would be able to make my difference and grow, and not be consumed by doubt. I would never be caught out again. I would never be undermined again. I would never need to cry silent bathroom tears again.

Golden Heart Inn

71

11 The gift of space and time

In Nettleton Bottom, my life changed direction and I started on a journey without a destination. There was no status I sought or needed, no office politics to navigate, no low-humming bureaucracy to slowly walk behind, and no strange origami shaped swan I had to fold my duck-like self into so that I could pretend to fit in and feel at home. It was just me with a softly spoken monologue and an uncertain acoustic set of tentative ideas without the big brand production, light-show or sound system; it was just me playing to small audiences mostly looking the other way.

I look back and wonder how on earth I thought this was a good idea, but at the time I knew I felt at peace with myself and in a world that was, even then, spinning ever faster that feeling meant a great deal to me.

At this point in the exhibition it is time to move away from some of the events that have changed my life, and to show you some of the wonderful people who have changed my life. However, I do not want to do this as if sharing an album of photo-shopped worshipful biographies which might be a little too soft-focus and Instagrammy for anyone to cope with. Instead, I want to show you some of the moments in time, like with Lawrence and Geoff, when the story seems to find the people to help me, just when I needed them most. These are the moments that have become milestones on my journey from Nettleton Bottom to now.

Before we get there however, I need to share a little about one of the threads that links my early life to the change of direction at Nettleton Bottom, and then on through into the place I find myself right now. In the exhibition so far, I have wanted to show you some of the things that helped to shape me, but until Nettleton Bottom I had not tried to make sense of these things, nor had I tried to consciously use them in my work. That would need to change if all I could rely on was being me, without any of the corporate trappings of missions and strategies and C-suite status to stand behind.

You will know already that I have never considered myself to be a brilliant lawyer, manager or leader; and I was never so secure in my credentials that I expected to win the day with just the force of my argument, personality or experience. Sadly, in some ways, I have never assumed I would be noticed, needed or valued. However, I have always known from a very young age that I have quietly noticed a great deal. To notice, it turns out, is a gift. It is the first step of change, a place of soft but significant influence and where kindness can flourish.

I think this started for me when I was just a boy and I used to stay with my grandmother (my mum's mum) to be some company for her after my grandfather had died. She lived in Westbury, Wiltshire and most days when I was with her, we would walk down the steep slope from her little house on the Butts, to the main road where there was a butcher and a general stores. It was a distance of a few hundred yards, but it would take for ages to get there. My nan seemed to know everyone, and everyone we met on this little walk wanted to stop and chat. Nan always had time for everyone; she never judged, never tried to rush away, and always left the space for whoever needed it, and for however long they needed it.

My life straddles this gentler, slower time, through into the rush and swirl of today's social media clicks, links and notifications that dictate our days, minute by minute. I have to say that I prefer the before to the now.

My nan's stroll to and from the shops was all about making time for other people. This has become for me, and I believe it was for her then, a way to be present in the world; our way to have a quiet purpose. To be in the moment for someone else, unencumbered by our own concerns, just listening, acknowledging and providing a necessary pause, is a special thing.

I noticed how, for my nan's friends, this seemed to be such a kind and caring gift, and it is one that has become more and more important to me with each passing year. However, I also know now, better than ever, that it only a gift when it is not filled with our own ideas and needs. The time we give to others is only precious when it is left free for them to step into and be themselves. To then share this space is a privilege. It doesn't matter if it is filled with important things or hardly anything at all. In the gift of unconditional time we honour the need we all have to be heard.

I can follow this thread all the way back from now to walking with my nan. It does not seem that much when it is said in just a few words, but it is what I do, and to some extent it is who I am. It is both inconsequential and vital; it is simple to say, but it is hard to do. It matters more than we can ever imagine, but it is impossible to measure. To make time for others is the difference I can make in this world.

In the chapters that follow, the exhibition will continue so that I may show you the portraits of some remarkable and wonderful people who have come into my life and made this thread of my career even more important to me. As a result of their love, care and kindness, I have been able to do more than I could ever have imagined when I was just a small boy walking to the shops with my nan, or even as the General Counsel in two major companies.

My final thought for this chapter is just a quiet reflection on the process of looking back. As I am finding for myself in the pages of these stories, to look back is not to try and make sense of the past, but to feel confident about the present. I look back not to judge myself, or to regret or to reassess, but simply to notice and to be thankful for everything that has helped me to arrive precisely where I am right now, still incomplete, still uncertain, but settled in who I am.

12 Leadership is about love

This next picture is one of my most precious. I think about it every time I work with new people; and in a way it has defined how I want to make my difference.

I have always felt that memories are more important than things and that memories made with the people we love are most important of all.

I do not want to portray this as being particularly virtuous or practical. In the end, in the society we live in, there must also be a financial and material reward to show for a working life and all our hard work, stress and contribution. Neither am I against an accumulation of things – a nice house, a nice car, nice clothes; but I am absolutely certain that what gives our lives colour and resonance and meaning are the memories we have made with people we care about deeply.

I hold this thought so tightly that I have come to believe that the greatest gift of leadership is to help people make the memories that will sustain them in their good times, but especially in their bad times. A bonus, or a promotion and a sense of purposeful career development might be important in the moment, but these things do not feed the soul. Being driven and acquisitive, doesn't add to our humanity, and pursuing business centric ambition alone, doesn't ground us in the responsibility to fulfil our potential using all the gifts we have been blessed to receive and which we should be encouraged to share with the world.

Leadership in the end is about love. A deep, selfless and profound sense of caring for others so that they may have the best opportunity to feel safe, to contribute in their way, and to explore their potential to make their difference.

I know that on the Pollyanna spectrum I may be at the far end. I also know that a working life is not meant to be an easy-listening picnic, or floating on a meandering stream in a Hundred Acre Wood theme park. I believe in striving for the highest possible standards and in having no exceptions whatsoever to the "no wankers" rule; but surely to goodness there must be more to work and life than our HR defined grade, our bench-marked salary band and our post code?

It has always saddened me that a work objective is most likely to be about defining a specific task by a specific date with a predictable and provable outcome. We tend therefore to channel our efforts into uninspiring binary activities; and sooner or later the only things left to motivate us are equally shallow incentives usually around money or status. Inevitably this pushes behaviours to a place where short-term business outcomes are seen as more important than relationships. People are then promoted on the back of their success in achieving short-term objectives and so people in leadership roles will often assume that driving towards even more narrow and efficient outcomes is the best way to succeed and is in fact their version of exemplary leadership.

But where is the love? Where is the joy in creating memories that will sustain people in good times and bad? Where is the understanding that leadership is not about the leader, but about the people we have the privilege to influence and care for. These thoughts are so much part of my work that when we wanted to create a leadership programme every element of it had to reflect these feelings. There would be no spurious strategy case studies, I wanted to make sustaining memories for everyone involved and to place love at the heart of our work.

The LBCambridge2 Leadership Programme took nearly six years to develop. Each element from venue, to menu, to speakers, to mentors, to delegates, literally everything had to fit. I can't tell you how much time I spend on this, but it can be measured in years, agonising over whether it was ready and if everything was in place.

Then in 2012 the first event was held and this is the most precious picture I want to share with you.

In the autumn before, I was heading to a busy coffee shop on Charlotte Street in London, I was a little late for a meeting with someone I had not met before. I had been looking for someone to be part of the programme who could help the delegates with their presentation skills. Before this meeting I had met and rejected twenty-two other possible collaborators. I didn't want anything cliched; I didn't want people to feel diminished; I didn't want to stick a camera in their face and make them feel embarrassed. I didn't want to train people to read the news or to speak at a political rally. If truth be told I knew very clearly what I didn't want, but I had pretty much no idea what I actually wanted.

It had just started to rain and as a result the café was exceptionally busy with pavement refugees, but I could see the person I was meeting and she had very kindly saved me a seat. This was the first time I met Fiona Laird. All I knew about her was that she worked in theatre and that a mutual contact thought she was brilliant. It wasn't much to go on, but after twenty-two failed meetings I was at least prepared to spend a few more minutes with another stranger, just in case this was the one.

Anyone meeting Fiona will never forget her. I let my cappuccino go cold listening to her stories even though I wondered what on earth she was talking about. I hardly said a word as we jumped from theatre work to voice coaching to body posture and well-being. It was a lot to take in, and I didn't understand most of it, but there was something mesmerising and wonderful in the pictures she painted in my mind.

I asked Fiona if she would show me how she worked with people and we agreed to meet the following week. I asked a law firm if we could borrow a meeting room and I met Fiona there to talk more seriously and in detail about her work away from the bustle of a busy café.

She asked me to take off my shoes and to lie on the floor. As a confirmed introvert and not altogether comfortable with hippy-shit, I suspected that this might not be for me, but there was something so compelling about Fiona's energy and commitment to her work, and I went with it. Within a few minutes I knew I had found the person I most needed to help the programme be what I needed it to be. Fiona understood that the programme was not about helping people to be leaders, but about helping people to be themselves; and to love being themselves.

As the first programme was coming to an end, we were in one of the stunning teaching rooms at the Moller Institute in Cambridge. We were overlooking the playing fields and a wintery sun was illuminating our space. Fiona had been working with the delegates on their voices, posture and breathing. She was helping them to understand the untapped power of their presence in a room and she was encouraging them to shine as themselves and not to wear the masks others might expect them to wear. The culmination of this work was for each delegate to share a Shakespeare sonnet with us.

Three or four delegates had been brave enough to go first and they were wonderful. It was moving and uplifting and beautiful. Then it was the turn of the next delegate. She had been hesitant about this moment from the beginning; and we all knew how nervous she was about any expectation for her to speak up. In this moment she was all of us who have ever felt that we have been unheard; however, we also knew that she was an amazing lawyer, with a beautiful soul and that her team adored her.

She stood in front us and in a calm, soft and resonant voice she spoke to us. Her sonnet quietly filled every corner of the room and touched our hearts. As her words came to us, silent tears started to roll down her face and we hung on every syllable she shared. When she finished, everyone in the room was rapt in silence, each of us with our own quiet tears. Then she turned to Fiona and said, "Thank you Fiona, thank you for helping me to find my voice".

As I tell this story I always cry. I am crying now writing these words.

I could not wish to share with you a more important picture about love, leadership and the power we all have to create memories with others that will last forever.

'The Faculty' an original design by Jon Honeyford

13 Perhaps there isn't an answer dear

In any exhibition, however carefully it has been curated, there may come a point when we start to feel a little overloaded. Perhaps there is just too much information to take in, and perhaps there is just too little time to reflect. When this happens to me, I tend to stop trying to be present with what I see and feel, and instead I start to look for broad, easy messages that I can pick up and carry with me as I start to rush towards the exit. It is as if I have had enough of exploring the meaning of something and want to head straight to the cafeteria with a few bite-size answers to take away with me.

In real life, we barely have time to make sense of anything, before the next thing, and then the next thing, and then the next thing, are upon us. Even in the best of times we are relentlessly and inexorably rushing up to and then beyond events, adventures, triumphs and disappointments. And all the while clinging to our lifebelt of hopes as we are swept along on the currents of our intertwining lives.

In the stories I have shared with you so far, I have taken mere moments of my life and even those are edited heavily. It is obvious therefore that it is not my whole story. All our lives are so much more complex, varied, detailed and problematic than any carefully assembled gallery of stories; and yet we all carry a sense of the exhibition of our lives that we prepared to show to others. Indeed, most relationships start as an escorted walk through our personal exhibitions as we share and receive the pictures and stories of our different lives.

In an exhibition, if it all gets a bit too much, we can choose to stop looking at the walls of carefully placed stories and seek refuge in the cafeteria. However, in our real lives, it is so much harder to stop being with our stories. There is nothing curated about the clutter of our realities and how this tests our strengths and weaknesses in equal measure and to the limit. There is no metaphorical cafeteria in which we can walk away to rest our overloaded senses.

Despite knowing all of this, there is still a great temptation for all of us to only notice the perfectly placed stories that others share with us, while residing in our own un-curated messy reality. It is because of this that I want to take you to a very specific fragment of a conversation with my friend and collaborator Kay Scorah who came into my life when I was putting together an experimental event that we called LawFest.

LawFest was a joyous mix of Jazz, theatrical improvisation, poetry, stand-up comedy, a narrated stage version of the Leveson Inquiry and the Bach Choral Society. It was held in Cheltenham where I live and we decorated the venue with bunting, hay bales and balloons. We drank beer and cider, laughed at the absurdity of it all and created a few memories that will stay with me forever. LawFest didn't become a regular event for us, but I hope to return to the idea one day. Its essence was to learn from all aspects of the performing arts, but where the audience performed and didn't just observe. It was messy, unrefined, incomplete and rather wonderful. In the late evening warmth of a summer's day, with a palate cleansing shower of rain to freshen the air, the LawFest audience melted away, a little bemused, heads wobbled, but smiling.

It was at LawFest that I had worked with Kay for the first time. She ran a contemporary dance workshop with a few brave lawyers revealing the emotions of their working day through dance. By all accounts they coped admirably.

I cannot do justice to Kay's extraordinary and beautiful career in a few words in this place. There are just too many wonderful versions of Kay Scorah, but they include the biochemist (her BSc Hons in Biochemistry from King's, London was followed by a year at the Max Planck Institut für Biophysik in Frankfurt studying the sidedness of anion transport across the erythrocyte membrane). Or the successful advertising executive, where (by the ridiculously young age of thirty-two) she had been on the board of directors of two London ad agencies and was a contributor and assistant producer on the 1990 BBC TV series on advertising and society, "Washes Whiter". Kay the entrepreneur set up her own business thirty-five years ago, HaveMoreFun Ltd, with the objective of helping individuals, teams and organisations to be their kind and creative best at work. She is a teacher and tutor working on the Oxford Strategic Leadership Programme at Said Business School, and with the Teenage Cancer Trust and at Modern Elder Academy which is a mid-life retreat centre in Baja California Sur, Mexico.

And there is still so much more, including the Kay who is the improvisational cook. In 2016 she published her "Essex Road Recipes", a deck of recipe cards designed to encourage people to cook from scratch and support local independent food retailers.

She is also the founder of an inspirational mentoring concept. Kay, told me that having learned so much from the young people that she had met through her work with Teenage Cancer Trust, and serving as an ally to a young Afghan as he worked his way through the process of being granted refugee status, and then working alongside a trans activist at London Southbank University, that she wanted to bring all their wisdom to senior business leaders. This became the Turning the Tables conference in London in 2020. And she continues to pair young people with business leaders in reverse mentoring relationships.

I could go on, but you get the picture. Quite simply, a film needs to be made and a biography must be written all about Kay. However, despite all of the riches I could write about, I want to focus on just one seemingly ordinary conversation, in one place at one time, and it's not even the most precious thing that Kay has given to me, which is (so you know) that she taught me how to listen. In so doing she changed my work and my life for the better, forever.

In addition to the work we do together at our events, I meet with Kay for lunch three or four times a year. Typically, we meet somewhere near King's Cross in London and over a pleasant light lunch we will talk about work, and families in the way that all good friends do.

In one of those conversations, I was describing to Kay some of my mentoring work and how life was pretty complicated for so many people. Not just their careers, but difficult family situations and the challenges we can all face from time to time with health, relationships and generally feeling overwhelmed. I said something like "And so it's hard to help them find the answers, but I think just being with them is helpful."

Kay has this wonderful way of receiving words as if the sounds they make really please her. She fixed me with a very knowing look and said "That's nice dear, but perhaps there isn't an answer. Perhaps there isn't meant to be an answer. Perhaps looking for answers is part of the problem."

We talked some more, but this was now the earworm for my day. I can hear Kay's voice right now and see the smile and the twinkle in her eye. It felt like Kay had touched a concern with a kind thought and in an instant it had turned into something so much more positive.

A bit like LawFest, perhaps our exhibitions (and our lives) are meant to be messy, unrefined and incomplete. Perhaps, when we let go of needing answers, we can enjoy being with our lives a little bit more.

That lunch ended with Kay telling me she would now walk home along the canal. She said she walked or ran along the canal most days, and in reply I said something dull about whether doing the same walk or run every day ever got boring. Kay gave me another knowing look "My dear, it is never the same run if you are noticing everything that is different."

Gustav Klimt,
'The Tree of Life'

'Cambridge Colleges' by Ian Weatherhead

14 Our beautiful bag of gifts and talents

I'd like to take you back to Cambridge to show you a picture of your talent. The picture is of a bag. It can be any bag you like, but it is one you should care about very much and one that you will always carry with you.

The LBCambridge event that Lawrence inspired and which we first ran in 2006, runs twice each year (pandemics permitting) in April and September. The event is held in the Old Hall of Queens' College, Cambridge. It was the original College dining hall dating from 1448 and is protected from the intrusions of the 21st century on one side by the River Cam and on the other side by a high brick wall with its repelling gates. To enter the inner sanctuary of the College and to be able to work in the Old Hall requires a short walk over the Mathematical Bridge that crosses the Cam into Cloister Court. Crossing the bridge is a mere twenty steps, but it is also a journey of several centuries. On one side of the bridge is the hustle and bustle of Cambridge as a place for visitors, casual punters and ice cream sellers, and on the other side is a tranquil closed haven of half-timbered buildings holding the outside world at bay and inviting all who enter to take their time for calm and peaceful reflection. Like no other place I know, this is where we can put down our cares and be open to share our thoughts and grow.

We gather in the Old Hall not to drive ambition, or to pump ourselves full of so called best practice ideology, or to puff ourselves up with tales of self-regarding deeds, but we gather to listen, and to share, and to pause, and to realise the power of the gifts and talents that we already own.

The event starts with a quote from Terry Pratchett's A Hat Full of Sky:

"Why do you go away? So that you can come back. So that you can see the place you came from with new eyes and extra colours... And the people there see you differently, too. Coming back to where you started is not the same as never leaving."

People have often asked me what the event is about expecting a sort of agenda of current topics and meaningful this-and-that on strategy and operational blah and woo. In truth however I have always found it hard to say what the event is about, because it is always about the people in the room on the days that we are there. In the past I have been reduced to saying that the event is a hopeful and kind pause where we ask everyone there to be their true selves, able to ask for what they need and to share in the process of helping others to find what they need too. As a message it is kind of ok, but I am not sure that it is a very compelling or informative on its own. As the years have gone by, however, and as generations of lawyers have walked across that bridge, I am now certain what the event is about.

I need to explain this carefully.

The most precious thing we will ever own is our talent; that mix of gifts, skills, experiences and judgement that we use every day to make our difference. It is like a bag that is packed with all that we need to take us safely on our career journeys.

Our bag of gifts and talents will take us through decades of work and along the way it will help to shape our hopes and fears, as well as providing the means for us to feel fulfilled and to provide the material means to look after ourselves and those we love and care for. It is a miracle of sorts that through our entire lives we will accumulate memories, feelings and behaviours that offer sustenance for our needs in the moment when we need them, and which we can share, pass on and receive back in equal measure as well.

This beautiful bag of sadness and joy, of good moments and bad, is the story of us and the narration of our dreams fulfilled and still to be fulfilled. It is ours, always ours, and we must look after it so very well. As a result, I have come to realise that the so called contract of employment (that mostly neglected document that frames the relationship with our employers) is not the most important contract we make with the organisations that hire us. The real deal is that we agree to lend our companies our bag of gifts and talents for a period of time on the understanding that these treasured things will be used well and nurtured kindly.

At the heart of being employed is the shared hope that we will use our gifts and talents to help our companies succeed, and in return our employers will help us to put even more experience into our bag. When we leave, our bag of gifts and talents will be heavier and more valuable that ever before.

Our responsibility therefore, is always to look after our bag of gifts and talents like it really is the most precious thing in the world that we will ever own. We must protect it from people and environments that diminish us or prevent us from making the difference that it is our duty to explore. We must also take care to look after our minds and bodies, because to feel less than our talent is to delay or waste our potential. While tiredness can be the honourable result of exacting and testing hard work, exhaustion is something else that is far more corrosive. Worst of all, being made to feel small, inadequate, or unworthy, can live with us forever if we are not careful. To lose our confidence or to be intimidated by people or workplace cultures, reduces and breaks what we carry in our bag of gifts and talents, and makes it so much harder for us to be ourselves. When we lend our bag of gifts and talents to others, we have a responsibility to notice harm and to value kindness. We must lend it well or take it back and move on to somewhere else.

Our journeys will always be fraught with risk as well as (hopefully) filled with joy. Once we have started to truly value our bag of gifts and talents, the next most important lesson to learn is that we should never try to travel far on our own. We need the love and understanding of our families, and others who care about us – our colleagues past and present, our mentors, bosses and friends. In turn we must learn to help them look after their gifts and talents, and we must know how to ask for their help when we need it too.

We need to find joy in kindness and not to be too precious about status, or the ephemeral brands we work for; we need to relish the journey with all its twists and turns, and to know we have all that we need, carefully packed away in our beautiful bag of gifts and talents. Then, when the time comes to look back, we will have travelled lightly without the burdens of others' expectations, or short-term and mean ambitions. We have our bag of gifts and talents, and it is all that we need.

A career can then be navigated gently, explored adventurously and shared generously. There is a quote that captures the essence of my hopes for us all.

"Let your boat of life be light, packed with only what you need – a homely home and simple pleasures, one or two friends, worth the name, someone to love and someone to love you, a cat, a dog, and a pipe or two, enough to eat and enough to wear, and a little more than enough to drink; for thirst is a dangerous thing."
Jerome K. Jerome, Three Men in a Boat

The walk across the Mathematical Bridge will never be a stride into a two-day course on how to be a better lawyer; it is however a few steps on our journey where we unpack our beautiful bag of gifts and talents to see all that we have, to repack it with love and care and then to head back out into the world, knowing we have all that we need to be utterly and wonderfully remarkable.

15 When the frame is more important than the picture

If you have come with me so far, you might like to know that we are now about halfway through the exhibition. There is still so much more that I want to show you, but like a real exhibition it isn't supposed to be a history of everything, just a few things that tell a story, and which I hope may help to affirm your stories too.

The corridor was unmistakably institutional – long, not terribly well lit and with a hint of "only be here if you are meant to be here." There were names on every solid brown varnished door, sometimes two names; but only small square windows to permit just a glimpse of the offices behind them. There was also the smell of floor polish hanging in the air above the worn parquet tiles, and every echoing step I took was triggering memories of school days at the start of term. The place felt solid and faded but not neglected. It was a place where budgets would be spent on higher things than colour schemes and soft furnishings. I was a little nervous to be so deep inside this world-renowned university, because the small boy from a small town that still thrived inside me was about to have a cup of tea with an eminent Professor with a national profile.

For a few months I had been reading Richard Moorhead's blog on Twitter and posting occasional comments back. In those days social media was a gentler place to spend time. Discourse was polite, amusing, supportive and often very kind. It had little of the angry, indignant, positional impatience that would overwhelm the space later.

I used to love the conversational threads that evolved on Twitter and the sense of generosity in them, whether they were serious themes or flights of whimsical nonsense. Richard was a generous Twitter correspondent, often taking points and debating them, and often contributing to posts others had made with care, clarity and humour. Twitter, then, felt like a safe place for me to be in my quietly introvert, non-academic, not-a-lawyer-anymore, softly spoken way.

Richard's writing has a wonderful quality to it. It sits in that place where it is both authoritative and sharply focussed but is not condescending or self-regarding. He somehow separates ego from evidence so that it is the argument that matters, but then he still wraps everything in a generous, accessible tone to welcome everyone to share in the thoughts he has so carefully laid out.

Reading his work on lawyer ethics, I knew I needed Richard to be part of my leadership work. And so, in that way of a shy teenager plucking up the courage to ask a girl to dance at the school disco, I wrote to Richard asking if he might meet me to discuss an event I was putting together. To my delight (and very unlike all my school disco rejections) Richard suggested we meet at UCL when I was next in London. So, here I was, two-thirds of the way down the corridor leading to his office and about to knock on his door.

In all the years following our first meeting I have grown to love his work even more. Of all the lawyers I have met, he has influenced my thinking on the role of lawyers in business and in society more than anyone. He is an evangelist, a teacher, a fearless challenger of settled and complacent orthodoxy, and above all he cares.

His work on the Post Office Scandal is typical. He has relentlessly and restlessly searched for the truth of what happened. He has sifted through the small evidential details that most people would have walked by. He has never shirked from posing the direct and uncomfortable questions that must be asked and answered. And I know he will not stop. Like Richard, we should all care now to respect the needs of those poor souls so calamitously treated by lawyers and executives who had the power and influence to behave better.

His approach is to painstakingly reveal the detail of his discoveries, like a legal archaeologist carefully brushing away years of accumulated mud to reveal an elaborate mosaic of half-truths, misconceptions, lies and incompetence. Richard cares about the detail, but it is far from being just an academic exercise, he cares about the people too. There is a picture in one of Richard's presentations of Noel Thomas, an Anglesey Sub-Postmaster jailed and ruined for a made-up crime. The picture is of Noel, taken outside the High Court in London following the hearing that cleared his name, and it reminds Richard of his dad. It's the jumper and jacket that does it, and every time Richard speaks to this slide there are tears in his eyes, as there are now in mine.

I am glad Richard cries because it makes the work more real, and it matters even more as a result. Real life isn't scenario planning in glass towers and boardrooms, and the truth isn't a commodity to be bought by the powerful and the wealthy.

Richard has taught me that if we truly care then we should feel uncomfortable with the great responsibility of our work. He urges us, deliberately and self-consciously, to do the right thing in our words, behaviour and actions. He has made me realise how blessed we are to have the talent and the opportunity to make our difference. He has also shown me that if we do not care about the people, then what is the bloody point.

When I tentatively knocked on Richard's office door, I had no idea I would be stepping into such a rich and vital world of colours and challenge, of ideas and questions, and of the urgency needed to hold back waves of complacency and privilege. He has made my work feel more important and purposeful, but most important of all, Richard has become a dear and precious friend.

As we move on from here, the image I want to leave you with in this part of the exhibition is of an empty picture frame, because sometimes it isn't the picture that matters the most, but the frame. Are we mindful, I wonder, of how we frame our advice? Are we curious how we collude with circumstances to create a plausible escape-lane for our decisions? Do we prefer to be seen as a cheer-leading business partner or as an independent critical friend? Do we therefore over-rely on the artfulness of the frame so that our blind eye can face the uncomfortable truth without seeing it and flinching?

Generations of lawyers have been force-fed a diet of finding a way to fulfil their clients' wishes and of never saying no. This might be part of the way we feel we should frame our job, but it is by no means the most important part. It is never our job to ruin Noel's life with our fine arguments and clever strategies.

Doing the right thing has never mattered more, and while it is a shared responsibility with everyone who has power and influence, there is no hiding place when a lawyer is on the wrong side of history. I am therefore forever grateful to Richard for his capacity to illuminate and help us shape our ethical frame.

I am also grateful for the chance to discover that Richard once lived in rural Worcestershire where his mum and dad ran a pub in my village. It is a strange but warming thought that his dad probably served me my Friday night pint, and even that the student Richard might have been there on some of the evenings when I was questioning my purpose as a lawyer with a quiet ale.

Through my friendship with Richard, I met his dad again in more recent times. He was a man whose values and frames could not have been more clearly defined, and who could not have been more proud of his brilliant son. I then had the sad but enormous privilege to attend his funeral. I tell you, I feel connected to Richard in so many ways that go far beyond our work, and I am blessed to know him.

All this began with me sitting in Richard's office in what might be kindly described as a county court waiting room chair, sipping scolding hot weak tea from plastic cup and quietly telling him of my hope that he might be part of my leadership event.

As we leave this part of the exhibition I have a request of you – please think about the frames that you use and not just the pictures of your life. Please also read about Noel's story to understand the grace and dignity of this man and his family. It is so important that those of us with privilege and power never lose sight of our duty to do the right thing.

Please know as well that knocking on a door on a dimly lit corridor will sometimes open onto a place of blessings that we could never have imagined would be possible.

16   A note of thanks

We are familiar with the idea of exhibitions as places filled mostly with pictures and objects, but sometimes the curator will place correspondence at the heart of things. The next thing I would like to share with you therefore is a simple note of thanks. I have written this as if it were a letter to my younger self, but it is definitely a letter of thanks and not of advice. Sometimes we are a little too quick to assume we must advise younger people with less experience than ourselves, when in reality we have so much to learn from them too.

Dear Paul,

I am a little sad that you didn't have this letter when you needed it most, when doubt overwhelmed you and when your confidence poured away. I wish I had been around to sit with you and to tell you that it would be ok. I am sorry I was not there. But you did indeed do ok my friend, and I am proud of how you coped. I see now that you had everything you needed, even then.

You are still with me every day. That feeling of wanting to step away from the crowd, of having a constant anxiety about fitting in, and of believing you have nothing important to say – none of this has changed or got easier. I may have thirty-plus years more experience than you, but the person I am now is still recognisably you. The one certainty of aging is that while we grow older on the outside, we still feel the same on the inside. Some things just don't change however old and gnarly and apparently wise we become. I will always be you – and grateful for this too.

Whatever insecurities and weaknesses we have, they are ours for a reason; each is a gift and they are all uniquely ours. When we are young our weaknesses and insecurities are something to hide and deny, but if our life is like a canvass, then using all the colours we have been given is essential if we are to create the most meaningful, important and cherished painting, and one that tells our whole story.

You hid your insecurities far too well, but what you were feeling was never something to hide and has become a deep and precious well of empathy and insight to draw on. Our weaknesses and insecurities help us to know how others might feel who are hiding part of themselves too. When we bring that understanding of ourselves out of hiding for others to see, the little miracle that happens is how much easier it is to help friends and colleagues who have not yet learned to value their own insecurities. Perhaps the reality is that there is no such thing as "imposter syndrome", but perhaps there is such a thing as "pretending-we-don't-have-imposter-syndrome syndrome".

However, I do not want this to be one of those letters that simply tells my younger self what I know now that I wish I had known back then. Instead, I want this to be a letter of thanks for what you, my younger self, have taught me and still teach me every day.

The first thing, and something I reflect on often, is that you taught me not to stay too long in any role. You moved when it felt right for you to move even when others cautioned you to stay. You moved to learn, to explore and to trust the adventure. A career is a privilege that will be full of gifts and opportunities, and if travel broadens the mind, so a career of changing roles and trying different things, encourages us to learn and grow. Our purpose is to make our difference in our way, and not to unconsciously follow the well-worn path, or worse to dwell in what might become comfortable complacency.

Moving on also helps us to realise how imperative it is that we hold our identity and values distinctly from the places we work. We should align with our work, but not embody it. You have shown me that we should never feel so valuable that we cannot be replaced, or feel so insecure that our gifts will not be welcome elsewhere. Confidence can be a fickle friend, but we will always have the opportunity to learn, grow and to make our mark wherever we are and whatever our role. Remember we always have our beautiful bag of gifts and talents, and we take it with us wherever we go.

I also want to thank you for your quiet contribution in groups and meetings, even when you knew that some people assumed you had little to say, and others did not even notice you were there. You knew that only saying what needed to be said was far more important than just saying something to fill a gap or to speak over others. You also knew that you had to be true to your introvert self and to find your way to make your contribution. Thanks to you, I realise how much more important it is to be someone who people want to listen to, rather than someone known for having a lot to say. You were the one who showed me how to influence quietly. It is something I see in others too, and thanks to you I can encourage those who do not wish to talk loudly or occupy the centre stage, to value what they offer and to help them find their way to be heard.

I see how you noticed that the first person to speak was often the first person to stop listening. As I have got older, the importance of listening has become even more obvious and precious. We live in a broadcast world where our loud truth can be used to silence others. To listen well however undermines nothing we believe in; indeed to listen well is to be confident about our own thoughts and feelings, and makes listening a generous gift for others who may not feel heard. It is also the best way to learn how and why other people feel what they do, and to realise how everything becomes a little easier when we are noticed and heard.

You showed me that to be a great follower is an act of kindness, and that to lead or manage someone is a precious act of followership if the leader is dedicated to the needs of others. You were also clear however that following well is different to being an unthinking cheerleader. Standing slightly apart, but nevertheless supporting, means we can be a critical friend and be true to ourselves. We must not let our organisations groom us to become compliant observers of their expediency. If the desire to fit in and to be accepted means we also lose sight of who we are and what we stand for, we diminish the opportunity for us to make our difference and we risk trading our values for status and money.

You have given me everything I needed to get me this far and I will always be grateful for the first steps you took that got me to here. This reflection is one I think may apply to everyone, because each day as I get older I see how we have far more to learn from those more junior and less experienced than ourselves. We rightly value experience, but there is such wisdom, courage, determination and creativity in everyone.

Grades, titles and hierarchies should never stop us listening and learning from anyone placed temporarily below us or make us unthinking and unchallenging about anyone placed temporarily above us.

Thank you. Take care. Paul xx

17 For good

I first went to the elegant and somewhat imposing Law Society building on London's Chancery Lane for my Admission Ceremony. I went with my dad (I was allowed to take just one guest) and I remember we were both slightly intimidated by the building. It felt grand and a little looming – somewhere between stately home and high church. The ceremony had the feel of a university graduation, but was also partly an induction. Although I had been qualified for a few months, I think this was the first time I truly felt part of the legal profession. I felt that I was now accountable for playing my part. I don't remember what was said exactly, but I do remember walking away that day and feeling that it was an honour to be included and to be given a chance to make my mark, however small that mark might be.

Over the years, indeed decades, since that day I have been a frequent visitor to the building. The black painted railings, the golden lions guarding the way in, and the steps up into the main entrance are all familiar and reassuring to me. I have often made the reading room my "London office" for the day and enjoyed the slightly faded grandeur of having such a place in which to meet people away from the bustle and brands of the city streets close by.

For a period of time, I was also a member of the Law Society Council and was elected by the Council to be a member of the main management board. The Law Society is often derided for being out of touch and irrelevant, sometimes rightly so, but it is also full of people who care and who bring their reality into view for others to understand better the issues, concerns and diverse interests that they feel passionately about. This is a profession, don't forget, with members that on

the same day might be representing the sovereign wealth fund of an oil-rich middle-eastern State, or who might be representing a shop-lifting child in a small northern town's magistrates court. From social welfare law to international inter-governmental arbitration, it is not easy therefore for the Law Society to speak with one voice or to make a difference across a profession that has long since lost any sense of having a common identity.

The portraits of elderly men in stiff collars looking down on me in the reading room all had a similar experience of being a lawyer in their time, but those days are long gone. Not having a common identity however, does not mean we cannot have a common purpose, and one that unites our roles and the kaleidoscope of interests we embody and represent. Thankfully, we will never again have an identity associated only with old white whiskery gentlemen in frock coats, however because of our diversity it is even more imperative that we unite around those things that only we are accountable for protecting.

The last thing I showed you in this exhibition was a letter to my younger self – a letter of thanks to an unnoticed and inconsequential man to whom I owe a great deal. As we are therefore looking at correspondence in this part of the exhibition, I would like to share with you an open letter to the leaders of the legal profession with some thoughts about what it should mean to be a lawyer today.

The self-regarding formula for such advice would typically expect me to address these words to a newly qualified lawyer, perhaps at another Admission Ceremony on Chancery Lane. That seems unfair; why should I impose even more on the youngest people in our profession and expect them to make a difference from the bottom of the ladder? That feels like easy, crowd-pleasing advice to appease the writer's guilt; and it gives a free pass to those who have climbed to the top already, who therefore have the real power to make a difference today. In the end, we should all practice speaking truth to power, not platitudes to the powerless, but those who lead should also carry the example for us to follow.

Dear Senior Lawyer,

If you describe yourself as a leader, may I ask you to work pro bono? Not "for free" but pro bono publico, for the public good.

I know I am nothing to you, I have no standing, and my time has largely gone, but from this end of the career path, I can see more clearly how trips and falls might lie in wait for you. I will not presume to tell you how to do your job, it is hard enough without me chipping in, and I know there are huge pressures for you to hit targets, to be a great business partner, and to be a commercially orientated supporter. However, I am also certain that our families, our colleagues and our communities need you to be a lawyer first before you are anything else, more than ever.

As a lawyer first, we need you to ensure that your colleagues and clients are in no doubt that your independence and integrity are important to you. We need you to have created the policies and processes for your team that reflect how important independence and integrity are to you. And we need you to show your colleagues that they can talk to you at any time if they feel even the slightest pressure to compromise their independence and integrity.

You have one of the most difficult roles to perform and I know you work hard and sometimes feel isolated and alone. I know you often achieve against the odds. It is hugely admirable, but please never assume that because you work hard and are well liked, that your personal values protect you from scrutiny. It will not matter that you are a popular and good person if things go wrong. What counts every day, while you are unambiguously reassuring your clients and colleagues how their interests matter to you, is noticing how you also reassure everyone else that doing the right thing is uppermost in your mind.

My advice to you today may sound harsh and seem to lack understanding of what you are trying to achieve, but it is heartfelt and shared with respect and appreciation.

If you work with less resource than you need, then you are a risk.

If you work when you are exhausted, intimidated or angry, then you are a risk.

If you are unsure if your client or employer understands the limits of what you can do within your professional duties, then you are a risk.

If you are not familiar with your own ethical rules and how they are currently interpreted, then you are a risk.

If you assume your colleagues are doing the right thing without knowing that they are, then you are a risk.

If you celebrate only victories, and do not celebrate doing the right thing, whether you win or lose, then you are a risk.

If you say or do anything behind the cloak of legal professional privilege that would embarrass you, your client or your employer in a court, inquiry or if ultimately published, then you are a risk.

If the financial incentives you have accepted alter the way you behave, then you are a risk.

If your reputation is dependent on a result, then you are a risk.

If you do not know or care how your advice or recommendations are being used by your client or your employer, then you are a risk.

The fashion for lawyers, for a generation or more, has been to underplay their role as officers of the court and to overplay the need to be the uncomplaining, commercial facilitators of whatever is wanted as long as it is legal. This is not just a corrupting mindset; it is lazy lawyering.

We are better than this. Society needs us to be better than this. I ask you please to be an inspiration for the next generation of lawyers to know that by following your example, they will become an example for others to follow too.

We can do this, Pro Bono Publico – now and always for good. Thank you.

Take care. Paul xx

18 For the stories

I have placed two letters in this exhibition so far – a note of thanks to my younger self and a reflection on leadership. I would now like to place a third and final letter in the exhibition, and this one is the most important of the three. It is for all the people it has been my privilege to mentor, but I would also like it to be read as a gentle encouragement for anyone who might need a little support and care.

Before I place the letter in the exhibition however, I would like to take you back a few years to a connection I made with two other members of my wonderful LBCambridge Faculty. I first "met" Martin Shovel on Twitter, noticing his political cartoons and how they were an outlet for his grumpy frustrations (and mine too). I dug a little deeper and found his Guardian articles on rhetoric and then I saw how with Martha Leyton they were speechwriters for some extraordinary people in public life.

I sat with the thought for a long time that their work and wisdom might play a part in my work too, but I didn't really know how. In my world there aren't that many makers of formal speeches and even fewer cartoonists. However, I knew there would be something special to find and I felt compelled to meet them. Without a plan or a proposal to share, I didn't want to waste their time, so noticing from Martin's Twitter feed that he was also a vocal Arsenal fan, I invited them both to a match. I hoped this would mean they would have a good afternoon even if we might not have an idea to discuss!

Meeting anyone in real life for the first time, when the only connection before has been online, is always odd, but thankfully they were reassuringly the embodiment of their Twitter timelines. Martha is the kind, gentle and measured guiding influence. Her wisdom is soft, principled and generous. It is offered unconditionally and with a quiet grace and care. Martin zigzags between ranty philosopher, music hall gag-man and a word-chef relishing every letter and sound a sentence can make. He has the tone of Alan Rickman, the acerbic observations of Woody Allen and the pathos of an old labrador.

Martin is the chilli heat, Martha is the cooling yogurt, and the combination is perfect.

We met and I loved them, but I still wasn't sure how we could work together. Sometimes an idea will come in an instant; other times, while we know there is something precious to find, we just have to give it time to be revealed. Then slowly but surely, and having tried a couple of things, we found the key to unlocking something wonderful. It feels obvious and natural now, but it needed to be found in its own way and in its own time. We all have a story to tell, a story that is ours and for the world. Martha and Martin help us to find our stories and then help us to tell them well.

And so, to the last letter in the exhibition.

My dear friend,

Thank you for the opportunity to be a mentor for you, to spend time with your thoughts and to sit quietly with your hopes.

I have learnt over the years that we all have our long list of ongoing and unmet needs, and we all have our hopes and fears that are the ever-present motorcycle outriders to escort our needs wherever we go. We live in strange times when it is possible to feel disconnected in a world of connection, and unnoticed in a world where everyone can see everything. It is so important therefore that we use the gifts we bring into this world to make our difference, so we may feel connected and seen. I hope that mentoring will always be part of how we do this.

Mentoring starts by understanding that being an adult is no more than the armour we place around the child within us.

Our armour is necessary and important protection, but we must try not to hide the child completely, because it is the child within who is always the best of us. This child is alive with creativity and possibility, hope and kindness. This child is generous and open, and will always want to shine. This child will never be uncomfortable to share feelings, seeking care and shelter when sad or alone, and able to bounce back from disappointment if supported, encouraged and loved. These are not adult skills, but what we learn from listening to our child within.

If we wear too much armour however, we stifle the child and we become just a grown-up shell of our potential and a speaking avatar of our synthesised needs. If we let the armour become too heavy to wear, the world will never see the difference we might make or the joy we might share. We must try to wear only the armour we need.

It has been a privilege to mentor you, to hear your stories, sometimes said out loud for the first time, and it has been an honour to hold the hand of your child within. I have learnt so much from you and I continue to draw on the grace and kindness you have shown to me. You have enriched my world and I am forever grateful.

Mentoring however doesn't stop when the conversation ends. When we learn to notice the child within, we can be guided forever by our true and authentic selves.

As grown-ups we learn to treat our vulnerability as weakness which we then try to hide behind our adult armour. But the child within wants the story to be told; and when it is, our vulnerability is no longer a weakness and becomes a new facet of what makes us real and special. It is like having extra colours in our palette of life experiences that we can use to create even more vivid pictures of our potential and contribution.

In case you think I might have gargled on some hippy-shit liqueur, I do not live in a world where if we think nice thoughts, nice things always happen. On the contrary, life can make it challenging and uncomfortable to be us, but pretending we can hide our vulnerabilities, means we carry them as extra weight and they hold us back.

Children love stories. They will sit enraptured by characters and storylines of implausible adventures; and no matter how often they are repeated, they will always find an unfiltered joy and inspiration in the tales they are told. When we tell our stories, we speak to the child in every one of us. When we listen to the stories others tell us, we become more invested in their triumphs and their struggles; we want them to overcome their problems and concerns, and we want them to celebrate their wins. Even more than this, their stories allow us to see ourselves and situations more clearly, more kindly and more hopefully, and they offer us encouragement to deal with our worries too.

To tell our story therefore is not a self-indulgent or self-regarding act. It is the way humans have always passed on their wisdom and made their struggle real. At one level, it is how we help others understand us better, to support us more and to value what we bring. But even more important than this, it is how we can help others find comfort and inspiration in their worlds too. It is our duty to tell our story, speaking from the child within us, to the child within everyone else.

Mentoring is a drop of kindness that will pay forward forever. We never forget the people who helped us, who listened when we felt unheard, and who saw when we felt unseen. We never forget how mentoring helped us to move on and to trust in ourselves again. And because we never forget, we are attuned to the struggle in others. Mentoring is always paid forward, passing on our forever stories so that they can find the need in others too.

Mentoring is a thread that connects so many people. It is a thread that starts with listening to our child within, to then encouraging our stories to be told, and to making those stories a gift of kindness for others to reflect on, learn from and grow.

Thank you for all you have given to me. Thank you for all you will give to others too.

From an original work by Julia Noble, based in San Francisco after moving from London and who has exhibited at Royal Academy of Arts, London. "My inspiration comes from the world around us, places, shapes, forms, and colours. The multiple processes that I use are intended to create works that convey messages of hope, resilience, and optimism, invoking feelings of joy in these challenging times." Ray is married to Julia

19 No one ever says "Ray who?"

We have now turned the corner in the exhibition and we are heading towards the exit. We are not there quite yet, but when we get there I promise we can rest a while in the exhibition cafe with a bun and a well-earned cup of tea – my treat, you will have earnt it. For now, however, I have a few more things to show you.

The last three exhibits have been letters. Letters tend to invite a quieter pause and a chance to reflect without the expectation of finding meaning. Reading a letter shuts out the wider world and takes us to a more intimate place where the voice of the writer meets the eyes and ears of the reader. It is a place where we can be lost in plain sight and transported without moving. When words are like this, they are like musical notes, and the feelings and memories they evoke take us away from the moment to somewhere personal, precious and uniquely ours. When words are like this, they can become a melody for an idea and a hook for a thought to return again and again whenever we need it.

And yet sadly the vast majority of the words we receive and send every single day, especially in our work, carry so little melody, or anything remotely tuneful that we would care to remember. So many words, and yet so little resonance that we can be overwhelmed with the pointlessness of it all; if we are not careful we can find ourselves living in a relentless soundscape devoid of joy, noticing only how empty vessels make the most noise.

We know this to be true, because we feel it every day, but the solution we have devised is not to seek meaning, or even to turn off the noise, but to say even more and spin those sounds ever faster and louder.

As we move away from the three letters in this exhibition, and the quiet calm they offer, may I please ask you to hold the thought that we should never move away from the power, beauty and joy just a few kind words can bring when we land them softly amid the din that we must all live within.

The next exhibit I want to show you is a client meeting room in the London Wall office of the law firm Osborne Clarke.

Lawrence and I had arrived to meet with executives and partners to discuss a possible collaboration that would see Osborne Clarke support The LBCambridge Programme. It is a journey we had been on before with other law firms and publishers. Like most conferences and events this support is essential and we have been blessed to work with many wonderful people over the years who have been generous and kind, and helped us to secure a sustainable foundation on which to build these fragile but wonderful experiences we are lucky enough to curate.

On this day in 2014 Lawrence and I were hopeful that Osborne Clarke would come on board, but we didn't know how they would approach the relationship and what they wanted to get from it.

The meeting room we used that day was plain and unprepossessing. The artwork felt like its purpose was to break up the wall rather than to carry a message or a theme. On top of a grey stationery cupboard top, white cups and saucers were lined up next to the ubiquitous metal jugs of coffee and hot water. A few shortbread biscuits were arranged on a plate and unbranded bottles of still and sparkling water completed the scene.

This room was quietly and unapologetically a place for a meeting, plain and simple, and definitely not an experiential installation for the ego of an interior designer that has got giddy with a budget and who believes a statement colour is more important that the words humans might speak when talking to each other. This was a room without an agenda; it was magnolia chic, and I loved its modesty and its willingness not to get in the way of conversation.

The meeting started and was polite and business-like. It felt positive up to a point, but also a little as if the handbrake was on. It felt like something was missing. It felt monochrome when we could do with a dash of colour.

Then, the door swung open and suddenly colour flooded in. Ray Berg, Managing Partner, was in the room – white t-shirt, faded blue jeans, serious statement trainers and fizzing with energy that was carbonated goodwill.

Ray couldn't enter a room quietly if he tried (I hope he never tries). "Hello, I'm Ray, have you done the deal yet?"

I think I said something like "Hi Ray, I'm Paul, this is Lawrence, we would love to do a deal, I think we just want OC to be sure."

"Great" said Ray, "Of course we want to do a deal, can't wait!"

Although I am pretty sure that what he actually said was,

"Great, of course we want to do the fucking deal, oops, sorry, excuse my French, I mean deal, can't wait. Has everyone got a coffee?" but that might be something I misheard.

Anyway, the deal was done and so entered into my life one of the most influential forces of nature I have ever met.

Ray might be like one of those pop stars that are unambiguously known by one name. I don't think anyone would ever say "which Ray do you mean?" or "Ray who? But this could, of course, be a negative. The possibility of straying towards diva-like tendencies would be a concern, as would the risk of a personal brand overtaking the business brand. However, there is nothing negative in knowing Ray.

Over the years since that first meeting in the magnolia chic meeting room in London Wall, the people of Osborne Clarke have been kind, loyal, caring, supportive, grateful, strong and nurturing. Each partner, associate, executive, manager and colleague has met us as people first. We have been vulnerable with them and sometimes they have been vulnerable with us. From the beginning it was never actually about "a deal" but about connection and relationship.

Writing this part of the story I wondered if Ray would like the exhibition, or if he would disappear at some point and seek out another can of Coke, but I think he would stay as long as the company was good. Ray loves people and he especially loves his people. I have never seen anyone who cared more with such an obvious passion for his colleagues. I won't drip with clichés at this point, but I will just say that if "love is all you need" is open to misplaced optimism, it certainly helps.

The contrast between Ray the man and the meeting room where we met for the first time makes me smile. Both confound the stereotype. The colour, contrast and creativity of a space should come from the people within it, and not the soft furnishings. Let the people shine and a tent can become a palace. Magnolia chic is permission to be whatever is needed, whenever it is needed.

Ray lives his life to an Ibiza dance music beat where the tracks of his days are about throwing light onto opportunity, kindness, making a mark, loving the success of colleagues and friends and wringing every drop of difference from a moment in time. Ray, I love you to bits my friend, thank you for all you have given to me and all you have shown me about kindness, leadership, friendship and caring.

In this exhibition I know I will revisit the magnolia chic meeting room from 2014 often. It will remind me always that it is always the people who bring the colour into the room to do the fucking deal.

20 The Pause

One of the reasons for inviting you into this exhibition was to create a pause.

Mentoring is all about creating a pause.

If we want to change something, or understand something better, the best way for this to happen is to enter a space where we have slowed things down enough to be able to notice and then reflect on what we have noticed. Noticing and reflection are the prelude for change and understanding; and the space for noticing and reflection is created when we pause.

Mentoring is all about creating a pause.

There is a poem I sometimes ask people to read a day or two ahead of a workshop, and this poem is the next exhibit I would like to share with you.

When I ask people to read it, I provide no explanation as to why I would like them to read it, but I don't suggest there is anything profound about it either. I just ask people to read it. The poem is this one, by Robert Frost:

Two roads diverged in a yellow wood,
And sorry I could not travel both
And be one traveler, long I stood
And looked down one as far as I could
To where it bent in the undergrowth;

Then took the other, as just as fair,
And having perhaps the better claim,
Because it was grassy and wanted wear;
Though as for that the passing there
Had worn them really about the same,

And both that morning equally lay
In leaves, no step had trodden black.
Oh, I kept the first for another day!
Yet knowing how way leads on to way,
I doubted if I should ever come back.

I shall be telling this with a sigh
Somewhere ages and ages hence:
Two roads diverged in a wood, and I—
I took the one less traveled by,
And that has made all the difference.

The sentiment described by Frost will be familiar even if the poem has only a distant memory from school days.

When my workshop begins, I ask people how they felt reading the poem.

I often have to ask the group the same question three or four times, because they will typically start to describe what the words mean, and not how the words made them feel. However, I want them to connect with a feeling rather than to describe what the words mean. When we eventually make the breakthrough and someone describes how they feel, we get to a much more interesting place for conversation. It is the start of noticing and the beginning of reflection.

I think most people attend a training workshop with low expectations of learning anything new, or helpful. I think many of us just hope that it will not be a total waste of time when we have so many other priorities and tasks to manage. I think at best we hope for a few moments to confirm or validate our own expectations, before we rush back to our priorities and tasks. It is a very low bar, but it is one that is still easy to bump into.

I do not run workshops however to teach people anything. How could I? I do not live your life; I do not have your boss. I do not have your knowledge, expertise, experience, cares or ambitions. I am not looking at the world through your eyes and I do not have to walk in your shoes. What could I possibly teach you in sixty minutes that would be useful? I suspect almost nothing.

I am not a teacher. I do not know more than you, and you will always know more about your world than me. People sometimes say about me that I seem humble and modest, but I have a lot to be humble and modest about. When I stand in front of you, I know before we begin that I can teach you nothing. All I can offer is to help you pause.

As I have said to you already in this exhibition, the answers to everything are all around us; they are not even hidden in plain sight, but they are with us and in reach – if only we could notice them, if only we could learn to pause.

So, please do not read Frost's poem and tell me it is about options and life choices; and please don't spend time wondering if the meaning is about taking the path that is less familiar. Who knows what Frost meant – maybe he was teasing us, maybe not; but anyway, it is not a draft contract that you have to renegotiate, or a set of rules to interpret. There isn't a right answer.

However, I do invite you to tell me how reading the poem makes you feel?

Do you notice needing to read it more than once?
Do you notice that you cannot read it quickly?
Do you hear your mind working a little harder to make sense of how it is written and wondering why?
Does the poem irritate you a little when it makes you slightly stumble around its construction? Or do you enjoy the search for something that might be hidden?
Does it let you think about your circumstances without pressing you to be happy or sad about them?
Does it make you wish you had a little more time to sit with beautiful words and relish their colours and rhythms, their landscapes and their portraits?

Whatever you notice, the poem is making you pause. It is slowing you down momentarily and letting your feelings quietly fill a space that you had previously left only for analysis, lists, jobs and pressure. It isn't giving you an answer, it isn't an algorithm, and it isn't a short-cut to help you go faster. It is just a pause, and mentoring is all about creating a pause.

21 The rage room

I was in Singapore with a client in December 2019. We were discussing her new team structure and the small but important shifts in behaviour that would be needed as the business evolved around her. I was also able to run a couple of gentle workshops to introduce ideas that would help her team make this transition a little more likely to succeed. For most of my short visit I was more reflective than usual about my good fortune to work with a brilliant leader and wonderful person, sharing, mentoring and learning together in a beautiful location, and in the kindest imaginable climate away from the middle of an English winter. As long as I live, the child inside me from a small town in Wiltshire will never quite believe that days like these are real.

On one of the evenings during my stay, the team had organised a social gathering which included attending a "Rage Room" where participants wearing overalls and safety goggles could let go of their passive-aggressive coping mechanisms to simply smash things up. Apparently, it is both fun and therapeutic, and I kind of understand why. The chance to beat seven bells out of an old TV while shouting the name of an irritating colleague, old boss or indeed an old partner, must be beneficial at some level.

Team building social gatherings for the people I work with however should be for the teams to enjoy and not for hosting hired help like me. At the end of a long day, I figure most teams will have had quite enough of my face and my words, so I prefer to leave them to their evening entertainment. Instead, I retire to find a view that I

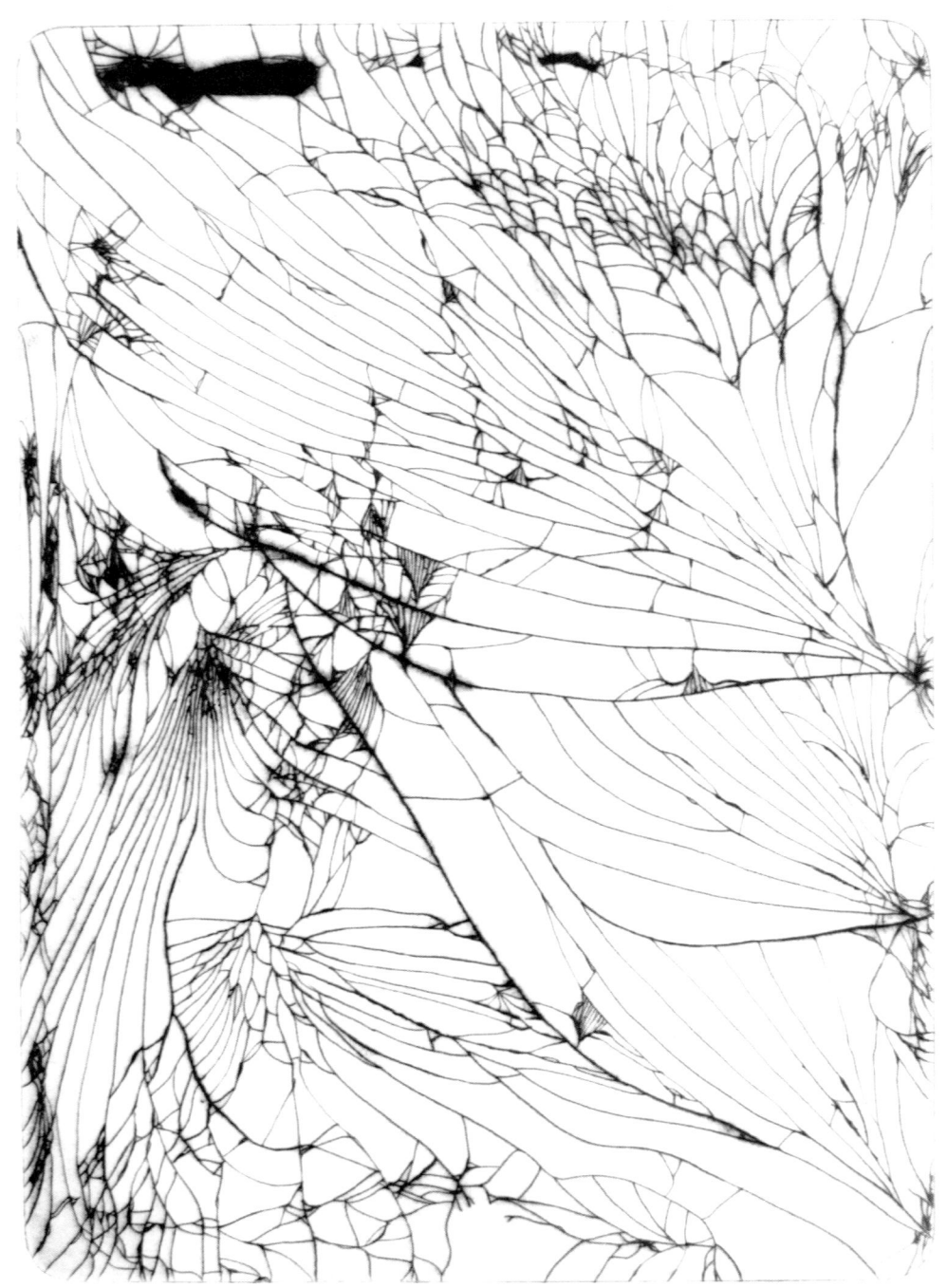

*'Shattered'
Drypoint etching
on paper by
Sam Hodge*

can recall on less good days, and linger there for a while with a cold beer to let my thoughts of gratitude settle quietly on my counted blessings.

The idea of a rage room however has stayed with me and in this part of our exhibition we will enter a metaphorical rage room where we can smash things up to our heart's content. I invite you therefore to think of the things you would like to place in your rage room; please take your time and reflect well, for this is your moment of destructive redemption.

Once you have placed your frustrations with care, mindfully and deliberately don your imaginary overalls, pull your protective goggles over your eyes and adjust the straps as only an expert assassin would do. Enter gently a realm of quiet meditation to summon the memories you will now wreak honourable vengeance upon. Then peacefully select your weapon of mass destruction, allow the adrenalin to rise like mercury in a heatwave, and finally like a whirling Dervish assailed by angry wasps, thrash the living bejesus out of your well-placed bugbears, and release your long-held unvented anger – possibly, if you have the head-space, do so as if filmed in high-definition slow-motion to the soundtrack of Apocalypse Now.

So, what is in my rage room?

What follows is NOT by any means my definitive list, but for now I hope it will serve to encourage you to have a similar space in your exhibition, so that from time to time we can all rage against the machine together.

Annual objectives that are disconnected from the roles people have and that take months to be agreed not because of meaningful negotiation, but because of bureaucratic indifference. Objectives which are then forgotten until the year-end bonus becomes a relevant possibility. Now suddenly the long-neglected objectives materialise like visiting far flung relatives who you think might have won the lottery; time to be nice to them, even though we barely recognise them and have nothing in common with them. Objectives should inspire; they should be relevant and lived, and matter – supporting a common effort towards a common ambition, and allowing employers and employees to achieve together. They should, but God almighty they hardly ever do.

Smart phones. I know they are extraordinary devices. They are miracles of innovation, bringing a whole world of worlds together in the palms of our hands. But you also know that we have become their slaves. They have taken the light and shade of our days and made us stare at small illuminated screens, rather than wonder at the limitless world of colours we have all around us. Smart phones open up a world of knowledge and connection, but disconnect us from the moments when we could be together in person living experiences in real time, in real life.

I accept that you may feel it is a step too far to actually smash up your phone, but if I concede that this rage room choice should not be imposed upon you, will you at least put your phones away in meetings? A meeting should be a shared experience where we reflect together, discuss, learn and decide together. What disrespect we therefore show each other when we cannot be without our technological comfort blanket even for a few minutes of human interaction. Imagine for a moment that it was not a smart phone we brought into the meeting room but a small pot plant that we proceeded to examine, water and prune while others talked around us. The level of distraction is the same and the absurdity is just the same as well.

While on the subject of meetings, I also want to smash up those meetings that sit in our online diaries like multi-coloured roadblocks preventing us from going anywhere meaningful in our day. The phrase "back-to-back" should be properly replaced with "block-to-block." Our working lives are not punctuated by meetings, but surrounded and trapped by them. A good meeting is an essential forum for good governance, decision-making, encouraging innovation, building consensus and sharing accountability. Yet far too many are limp, directionless and dull meanders around a half-remembered purpose where we all contrive to waste an equal amount of time together in conspiratorial ineptitude. Meetings fashioned from lazy thinking and the expediency of pressing a few buttons in the hopeless illusion of making progress. A meeting should be an event, not a shared brain-fade.

Another thing I want to smash-up are window-dressing wellbeing policies. Far too many colleagues are still punished by workplace cultures that undermine their mental health. Bullying, misogyny, bias and careless unkindness are everyday experiences enacted in plain sight. Our well-intended policies to prevent these things will not help if we do not address the behaviours, incentives and cultures that facilitate these things. Indeed, without addressing culture, the policies become the invisibility cloaks for casual leadership to disappear behind. Leaders must stand in front of the values they proclaim and show they are real, not stand behind them providing the cover for them to look the other way. A policy without action and leadership, is at best a field hospital in a war zone. We should want to stop the war, not just patch up the wounded.

Unkindness is the next thing I want to smash to smithereens. I just don't get why anyone would be unkind. Leadership is such a privilege, and the privilege is to serve the needs of the people we lead. Power imbalances are hard to navigate, but it becomes impossible when we don't care, when we are thoughtless about our decisions and actions, and when we elevate our needs above the needs of others. Unkindness is sometimes deliberate, but more often it is a product of neglect. The space between good intentions now overgrown with the stinging nettles of our indifference. The frustrating thing is that kindness is just so easy and requires no budget or resource or even a plan. It simply starts by being interested, in listening, encouraging, sharing and caring. We don't need to go on some sort of Harvard inspired kindness masterclass – we are all born with the gift of kindness.

Sadly, however it seems to me that we too often put kindness on the shelf labelled "nice to do when all is well" and some leaders have conflated kindness with indulgence and lax standards. I'd like to smash that notion too. Do we get anywhere worthwhile, sustainably and joyfully by being unkind? Leadership can sometimes be really tough, and hard decisions make for hard choices which are not always good news for everyone; but kindness should still guide us to make those decisions the best they can be, and their consequences should always be considered, thought-through and caring. Leadership is the best vehicle we have for showing the power of kindness. Unkindness is to trash that potential and diminish everything and everyone around its insidious impact. Unkindness therefore will always be in my rage room.

Time now I think to shut the door and move on; we should not dwell too long in places that make us sad or frustrated, but I thank you for passing through and indulging my need to show you this space. Time now for something altogether more uplifting.

22 The Blessings Room

From the room of rage, I want to take you now into a room of blessings. This is a space to be with our quiet and most precious thoughts – no noise or mayhem, no smashing things up – and the calm that comes from feeling protected and being at peace with ourselves.

I hope in all our lives we will have an abundance of blessings. However, I also know that this may ebb and flow. In some moments we will feel pain, feel unloved or feel alone; indeed, we might suspect that the rawness of the moment is scraping our blessings away. Even then, I hope we might find some solace in a place that we have made with love and happiness, and that can nourish our weakened state. A room of blessings which we have built to go back to when we feel a little lost.

This is the part of the exhibition I will come back to time and time again. I will return not just to remind myself of people, ideas and moments that have shaped my life, but also to bring in new people, new ideas and new moments. It is not a place to preserve things, like a museum of dusty old memories, but a place to re-energise us. It is a lifelong personal power pack, where the renewable fuel is love, kindness and hope, and where we may find the confidence and courage to be ourselves, and to go again.

The essence of everything I have written about so far will be in my room of blessings, but to talk about some blessings and not others, might create a false impression of importance and priority. You will know this exhibition can only be a small window that I have opened to let in a little light. As Martin Shovel and Martha Leyton would say, it is but a story written on a grain of rice. Far more importantly, therefore, it is all our stories that the world must see, feel and hear. This is how we learn, how we grow, how we look after each other, how we mentor and how we are mentored. It is our collective wisdom and goodness that will change the world, so we have to pool our blessings and tell our stories. Remember the answer to everything is all around us in plain sight. Our blessings can then be the soundtrack to the paths we take.

A room for our blessings is a lovely way to pause gently, to notice them and to feel replenished by them. However, it takes time to reflect properly and it takes time to notice. I do urge you therefore, if you can, to sometimes step aside from the swirling winds of the moment, and to find a sheltered place for your thoughts to settle. I know from my mentoring work that we are not always very good at framing

things kindly, and as a result we do not always notice all that we have and all that we bring. I will therefore share one blessing to show how we might relish, even more, some of the things that make our lives special.

I hope we can all include friendship in our room of blessings. Friends from when we were at school, from work, from the school gate waiting for our children, from our hobbies and interests and networks. But, perhaps there is another blessing in friendship to notice – that of the unlikely friendship. The friendship that comes from the intersection of lives on different paths, but which then opens up new worlds and new perspectives we might never have seen or loved.

I was first aware of Carolyn Kirby when I joined the Law Society Council in 1999

Shortly after my first Council meeting she was the elected Deputy Vice President and was on track to become President two years later. I didn't know her at all, but I knew she was a judge and, in my small-boy-from-Wiltshire eyes, my unconscious biases would have made her seem quite formidable.

The very first time she spoke to me was shortly after I had been elected by the Council's membership to be their representative on the main management board. I thought she was about to say something supportive and welcoming, but instead she told me how disappointed she was that someone very special on Council, who had served for many years, had not been elected (because of me). It was one of those moments that leave you feeling a little unsure what to say. She wasn't cross with me or in any way undermining my credentials, but I didn't have the words to reply.

I reflected afterwards that it wasn't harsh or pointed, but how I hoped one day I might have a friend like Carolyn who would be my advocate when I was in need of a voice to speak up for me; someone who would step in to make a difference and who would do so out of love and caring, not for any self-interest they might have. I was lucky to meet Carolyn on that day, and it has been an enduring blessing ever since.

For the next two years I watched how Carolyn became a brilliant leader of the Law Society; especially in the way she always stepped in with courage when most of us only observed. To speak up for people and causes, because it is the right thing to do, is her second nature. She was also a brilliant executive – in my whole career I have never seen anyone facilitate or chair a meeting with as much control, good humour, grace and care. Every item heard, every contribution valued, every decision reflecting the room, every point of disagreement respected and treated on its merits. It was a wonderful thing to watch and Carolyn was (still is) brilliant at it.

I suspect that I have learnt more about executive decision-making, reading a room, and building consensus from her than anyone else in my career.

I also got to know the other Council member that Carolyn was referring to in our first conversation. She was right about him too. He was a wonderfully gifted lawyer and a generous, kind and passionate leader as well. Despite the result of the main board election, he accepted me with charm and gave me so much good advice as I made my way at a senior level within The Law Society. It was yet another blessing for me to learn how magnanimous someone can be when events do not always turn out as they might have hoped.

Carolyn was the first woman to become President of the Law Society. It was, and always will be, an historic moment for the institution; Carolyn's approach however was never to rest on this milestone, and she dedicated herself to every meeting, every cause and every person who needed her time. The Law Society is much maligned, but from the inside I saw this particular President's extraordinary dedication and selfless duty, and always carried out with her usual humour, grace and care.

To be a serious person, embodying what it means to represent something bigger and more important than oneself, and yet not to take oneself too seriously, is rare and precious. We should value such people when they emerge, because they are people to follow. It was genuinely a privilege to notice someone who simply wanted to serve and who did so with a gift for inspiring others to walk beside her.

As the years have gone by Carolyn has become a wonderfully kind and generous friend to me and to my world of work. She is a mentor in every sense of the word, an exemplar of kindness and generosity, and I have loved learning so much from her. It will be a story for another time, but Carolyn's love and friendship means more to me than I can easily say. She has rescued me more than once, and I will be indebted to her forever.

A few years after her presidential year, Carolyn had become the Chair to the Council of Governors for Cheltenham Ladies' College. The Ladies' College is an institution as prestigious as Eton, but without the baggage of educating so many bloody awful politicians. Carolyn asked me if I would consider joining the Council and at first I was very reluctant. My personal politics are more socialist than privileged, and I was for many years a member of the Labour Party. It seemed to me to be a non-starter. However, Carolyn asked me to keep an open mind and to understand the College, its ethos and its example, before I made a decision.

What I found was inspirational leadership, especially in the pupils, and in so many of the teachers and staff. I also had the privilege to be part of a selection panel appointing a new Principal, and to the day I die I will never forget the feeling I had when the successful candidate made her presentation on her hopes and ambitions for the value and importance of education and life-long learning. It was a pinch me moment of joy and inspiration.

There are so many moments where, thanks to Carolyn, I have witnessed selfless, kind and inspirational leadership – all done without expectation of reward or recognition.

Carolyn is, in some ways, my most unlikely friend. Not because our values are different or because our hopes for the world are not aligned, but simply because we met by chance at the intersection of two very different paths. What a blessing this has become and her friendship is even more precious as a result. It has been a joy to be close enough to see her positive influence on so many people and on the issues that matter to her. A true blessing indeed. May we all have unlikely friends who share with us moments that we would never have experienced otherwise and who help us to grow and be better people for knowing them.

And may your room of blessings be packed full of reflective joy in the people you know, the moments you have shared with them, and in the support that you have felt with them.

Carolyn, thank you for your love and friendship; you will have mine forever.

23 The rooms beyond blessings Part One

A room of blessings feels like the best place in which to reflect as we move towards the end of the exhibition and this story. What could be better than to pause in the room where all the things that really matter to us have been placed safely to see and to hold whenever we need to feel their warmth and encouragement?

You may remember that we began this story twenty-three years ago in a café on Baker Street in London meeting Lawrence for a coffee and discussing a report that would change my life forever for the better. I can tell you now that we will end this story with Lawrence in a different café, this time in a Cotswold village twenty-three years later.

Before we get there, however, I would like to take a moment to reflect with you on your story.

I hope you will have known for a while that I have not wanted to take you around this exhibition to tell you my story, but to show you yours. I am not writing to see if you notice me, but to ask whether in my words you have noticed the light that you shine. I want to explore this further with you before the exhibition ends; because I need you to walk away holding your story, not mine.

My work as a mentor began long before I even used the word or knew its meaning. It was simply what I did when I gave someone a little time to care about some of the thoughts and ideas in that person's life; to listen to their words, as they wanted to share them with me. There was no expectation of anything changing as a result, or of handing back little parcels of perfectly wrapped wisdom; it was just the act of being still with the thoughts of another fellow traveller. A bench on which to rest for a few moments before the long walk starts again.

In those early days, I realised that to pause, to listen and to care had a value, and I settled comfortably into a way of thinking that this was enough. For some people I met, the sadness was that their working lives were so depleted of anyone giving them any time in this way, that there was no need for me to do any more. They were grateful enough.

However, as time went on, and as some of the stories I heard became all too sadly familiar, I knew that just to listen would not be enough. I needed the people I listened to, to begin to feel the power of their own story, first to help themselves and then to help others.

One of the most inspirational people I have ever met is a former soldier called Justin Featherstone. Justin's career in the Armed Services is the stuff of action movie film scripts, but it is not those stories that stay with me so much as the soulfulness of his manner and the poetry of his words. Justin has become integral to all our programmes and he is for me the embodiment of values-based leadership. In a tumultuous world, what Justin stands for and lives by, is a North Star for all of us lucky enough to know him.

I first met Justin on the recommendation of a mutual friend in a small café in Taunton in Somerset. (Maybe for my next book I should write about cafes rather than exhibitions!) I was looking for someone to fill a gap in our leadership programme. However, I was not looking for wall-hung cliches and action heroes, what I needed was someone to show us the power and potential of humility, and who could show us that our vulnerability, instead of making us weaker, was where our humanity to others begins.

I have never believed that leadership was about status or hierarchy. I do not believe it is about daring do, and I do not believe it is the preserve of the self-confident egotist who can easily put their self-regarding decisiveness above reflection and kindness.

Justin's story is so powerful because with his background he could easily have chosen to skim anecdotes across the surface of his boys-own adventures; and he could have puffed himself up to blow rollicking good yarns into our small, intimidated lives. It would fill a slot at a cheap cologne sales conference for sure, but it would only be a sticky sugar rush that would then leave us empty and unfulfilled.

Instead, Justin confounds the all-action stereotype. He is a quiet man. He is also a man of beautiful words; he has a way of holding an idea for us with the same care that we would hold a child's hand. He presents not as "look at what I have done", but as "look at what we might do together". Above all he starts from understanding where everyone is beginning their journey with him. He then comes back to that point with each of us, sits quietly with us for a while to just be, and then says, "when you are ready, let's go together."

It is a style of leadership that is understated, almost unnoticed, but then it is also profoundly affecting. It is the essential style of leadership for our times, because our families, our communities and our planet do not need the disposable spin of slogans and cliches, but to harness the power we all have to care a little more for each other.

There have been (too many) days of unimaginable violence in his life, but the calm assurance of sitting next to him when there is no need to speak unless it is something you want to say, is powerful and of itself is almost overwhelming. I think it is a kind of love; a loving respect for a person in a moment when the only thing that matters is that they are worthy of all the time they need for their words to be heard.

What Justin has shown me more profoundly than he may himself have realised, is that mentoring is so much more than just listening. It is an act of honouring an individual as a complete person, without judgement or comment, and to offer them your entire unconditional attention.

The mentor should never assume their role is that of the wise interpreter, but the mentor should always be the person who slows things down enough for our words to have the space to find meaning, for silence to move us and for our thoughts to rest in the light of another's kindness.

As I have reached that part of my working life when there is far more to my past than there will be to my future, it is impossible not to reflect and to notice. In part that is why I have written this story. I have wanted to show you how moments shape us, but more importantly to show you how the answer to everything is all around us, if we can only take the time to notice and to reflect.

In the pages that follow I will share a little more of how I believe we can help each other to navigate and narrate our own stories, and to notice what we have placed in our own exhibitions without even realising that this is what we have done.

The exhibition of our story is the foundation on which we build the difference we will make; it is what gives us hope even in our setbacks and gives meaning to our triumphs. The exhibition of our story is how we can be present enough in the moment to see that the answers are indeed all around us in the stories of others. And, as I have already said a little earlier, we will explore this further before the exhibition ends; because I really do need you to walk away holding your story, not mine.

24 The rooms beyond blessings Part Two

Each part of this exhibition has been a gentle request to pause in front of something I have placed there for your reflection and mine. Some of these things are small and not obviously consequential, but everything has been placed with as much care as I could give them. I have done this so that you could see them clearly, understand them, and know their value to me.

As you will have gathered it is far from being a showcase for Pollyanna glassware where everything is always half-full. That would be to make my story just another heavily edited and immaculately primped Instagram page. However, by placing things in my imagined exhibition that tell just a little of my story, I hope it may offer the opportunity for you to notice your story too, and to realise that each of our stories is so much richer than we think, more powerful than we have realised and, above all, that every story deserves to be told.

Most of our lives are hidden from each other in plain sight, but none are ordinary. When we notice our own story, and see how it has shaped us (and how it has influenced others) it is easier for us to accept what has been and easier as well to influence what is to come. Our back-story will contain the narrative of our potential. When we know how to tell our story well, and know its value, it becomes the platform for the difference we will make in the world.

The rooms we have not yet filled in the exhibition of our story, the rooms beyond blessings, should therefore give us hope that we will step into any given moment and make a difference. Whatever we can do, however small and seemingly

consequential it may seem at the time, that small thing might just be the origin story for something that later deserves a special place in our exhibition; how wonderful would that be and how important therefore to try.

We can all hope for a kinder world, where the differences between us are not what we fear and want to hate, but what we celebrate and want to love. And yet, in the world today, where so many have to endure unimaginable pain and suffering, it can feel that all we have left is to wrap ourselves in despair, where kindness feels pointlessly out of reach and hope is a place we have forgotten how to find.

We all know that in our own darkest days of great personal loss and sadness, when we have felt crushed by the weight of grief or the hopelessness of ever finding a way to cope, that we were rarely revived by well-intended clichés and platitudes, even from people who love us dearly. We also know that our existential despair for the pain and suffering in the world often leaves us gasping to make sense of what has happened. But in the end it is beyond our comprehension, and all we have left is an unsatisfactory vocabulary and eyes that need to look away. Sometimes, when darkness descends, it is better not to pretend there is light.

Terrible things must be given terrible names and the last kindness left to any of us is not to diminish or judge another human being's suffering and pain. One day however, as dark as the darkness feels today, some light will return. In the meantime, however long that may be, we must not ignore the power we have to make our own small difference to something or someone today. We must try not to despair, even in the darkest of days.

I will hold tight to that thought for now.

25 Nearly there

As we will soon be leaving the exhibition, this is a moment to perhaps notice a few things that I hope we may carry quietly with us even as we step from the peace and calm of this space and back into the pavement throng of our busy lives.

As always, the things I would like you to notice are not shared as unarguable truths, but simply as passing reflections for you to hold lightly, and only for as long as they help you to pause.

All exhibitions in our major galleries and museums will have the inevitable "retail experience" encouraging us to buy a memory before we make our way towards the exit. However, in my exhibition there is no retail experience; there will be nothing to clutter a shelf or postcards to put in a forgotten drawer with images that hardly touch the sides of depicting the joy of what we have just seen. We all know, I think, that there is no hope of finding something again that once truly moved us when that feeling has been reduced to a blurry image on a tea towel.

It is the tokenism of our busy lives that makes me anxious. I am anxious that we make sense of confusion and complexity by over-relying on the things we agree with, while denying the things that we don't. I am anxious that we seek answers that are not designed to address the problems we face, but to give us false comfort in the opinions we hold. I am anxious that that we offer lazy support to those who agree with us, when in our hearts we know we learn more from challenge and debate. I am anxious that we have turned our humanity into a retail experience – where we offer each other cheap imitations of things that should never be bought or sold, excusing us the trouble to grow, explore, change and care; and instead filling our lives with the soulless memorabilia of easy to spout half-truths.

So, the words I have written here, and which you are kindly reading now, should only be held lightly and only for a while. I am one in seven billion on this planet which makes me both unique and pointless at the same time. I write these words therefore not to displace yours, or to hold my opinions higher than yours; but I write them to honour your thoughts and to ask that you allow your thoughts to be carried lightly by others as well.

I believe with all my heart that there is so much more goodness to find, to cherish and to share than we have discovered in our lives so far. I believe that kindness is an energy source that will never be depleted and is renewable in everyone and in every small act of caring. Above all, I believe we find our way in this world when we let ourselves notice the difference that only we we can make.

When we step back into the pavement throng of our busy lives, jostled and shoved by strangers, unable to see clearly the path we are on and sometimes carried away from where we would like to be, I ask you not to hold my thoughts, but to hold your own with all the care you can find to look after something so precious and unique. Allow them to guide you and to speak up for you, because that is how we make the world a little better.

The exhibition of our lives should not finish with a confection of cliches on poorly made fridge magnets, but in the way our reflections give us a pause for kindness even in the middle of the pavement throng.

It is almost certainly pointless to think we will change the world on our own, but I am certain we are all uniquely placed to make our difference if we seek out undiscovered goodness and trust that we will never, ever run out of kindness.

Beyond the exhibition and before the exit there is always a café. A place to refresh, rest a little and reflect on what we have just seen, but also a place that sits at the boundary of two worlds – a place between curated calm and the more chaotic spin of our real lives.

You will have gathered that I very much like the idea of a pause and the opportunity to notice. The time we make to do this is never wasted. Galleries and exhibitions are brilliant for this – a place where the rush and clamour of the outside world is suspended just for a while and replaced with a quieter, slower and more reflective pace that allows us to see and feel a story that might otherwise have gone unnoticed.

When we tell our story well, when we truly see its value and love what it means, it will speak for us and it will speak for others too. As a society, as a team, as individuals, we all grow stronger and more powerful, and see more opportunity when we can see, feel and relate to what others have achieved. It is so much harder to imagine the contribution we might make if we do not see ourselves in the stories that others have told before us. Stories are like pathways illuminated with the light that others have left behind so that we might step forward with more confidence and determination to make our own unique contribution.

By telling our stories we therefore help others to be what they can be, but we help ourselves as well. We slow down the swirling whirl of the unrelenting moment, so that we may rest a little away from the din, knowing that we have already travelled well. The energy we need to go again is not summoned in the moment from thin air, it is in our story, embedded in all we have achieved before.

To tell our story is not to boast or to say, "look at me," it is to link our past with our present, to make a connection with those who have inspired us and to offer the hope that we might inspire others too. The only certainty when we do not tell our story is that none of us will make the world a better place by pretending we have nothing to say.

To pause also gives us a better opportunity to see the moments that make everything worthwhile. In my work I spend a lot of time with busy people talking about purpose and fulfilment but knowing that their day-to-day commitments and the onrushing sound of an overwhelming workload, mean we focus more on coping than thriving. To pause is not to indulge ourselves when we should just "keep going". Neither is it a luxury to sometimes step away from the joyless austerity of our diary which offers so little support or kindness. Pausing is necessary if we are to make sense of our place in the world. Pausing is necessary if we are to relish the gifts we have, and to use them well.

If I were to describe my personal purpose as it feels to me today, it is to help others to pause so that they might see the moments that make everything worthwhile for them.

The café at the end of the exhibition is where we prepare to re-enter our real world. In this exhibition I hope we may have seen some things that moved us a little, that made us think, and that have hopefully caused us to pause, if only for a few moments. I hope we have found some peace and inspiration in a place designed for reflection.

And now we are in the café, scanning for a table that might be free, deciding if having cake this close to lunchtime is still ok, and already noticing that the calm of a curated pause is subsiding. Here the background noise is louder, the light is harsher, and there is a slight sense of loss seeping into our thoughts as we prepare to get back to our reality.

We are nearly there, nearly at the end, but this liminal café space is precious too and we should not rush our drink (or cake) before our restless world demands our attention again.

When we move through any exhibition our role is partly to notice, partly to reflect and partly to ask ourselves how we want to take the experience with us when we leave. I say this not to make everything sound profound and vital, but just to make sure we have slowed things down enough to see the blessings in our reflections, if there have been blessings to see.

As we sit in the liminal café, a pause between two worlds, I would like to reflect with you that my work since meeting Lawrence in that café on Baker Street twenty-three years ago has been in a liminal space. I work with people between careers, between moments of stress and joy, between old certainties and new beginnings; but more than that, my world is in a space mostly unnoticed and unseen. As I say, my purpose is to help people navigate their own liminal spaces, not to rush through these transitions, but to make them an intentional pause where we see things in a different light and in new colours, so that we may notice more moments that make everything worthwhile.

I love my liminal world; I love that I can support wonderful people without being in the way of their success, but to be present enough to help them hold their vulnerability when it might become momentarily too heavy to carry on their own. My world is a constant and wonderful blessing.

Before we leave the café, I should acknowledge with you that not everything I value in my world is here in the exhibition. I have only mentioned a few of the people who inspire me every day, but there are so many others not mentioned who do this too. There are also places I have been and experiences I have had that shape my world and the way I gaze upon it, but too many to include in one small exhibition space. The story we tell, is only ever part of us, it is never all of us; and like any exhibition mine is a curated insight into just a small part of my world. As Martha and Martin would say, it is but a story written on a grain of rice.

There is never just one story to tell about any of us, never just one way to see our lives, or one way to know what matters to us. There is never just one exhibition, whoever we are and whoever we share our story with.

In time I hope to write much more. There are things I have not yet found the words to share, and stories to tell that I hope others may rest within for comfort and some support. However, most importantly of all I need to write more so that I may celebrate the work of so many others who have changed my life for the better (and for many others too).

For the moment, we are nearly at the end of this part of this story. If I were to sit here with you now in my liminal café, in the space between my exhibition and the bustle of our hectic lives, I wouldn't ask you what you thought of my exhibition, but I would ask you how you would like to curate yours. I know it would inspire me and I hope it might inspire you too. Our stories are the foundations for the blessings in our lives today and contain the hopes and the inspiration for the difference we are here to make in the world.

My exhibition is not about my story, but about how you might tell yours.

I BELIEVE WITH ALL MY HEART THAT THERE IS SO MUCH MORE GOODNESS TO FIND TO CHERISH AND TO SHARE THAN WE HAVE DISCOVERED IN OUR LIVES SO FAR.

26 The last chapter, back to the beginning

Thank you for being with me as I have taken you around my exhibition. Your company has been so lovely and I am truly grateful for your support and encouragement. We are now at the end, and it is almost time to say goodbye, but before I go there is one last story to share.

In many museums and galleries the entrance and exit to the main exhibition space are often next to each other with a shared milling area in between. A circular curated route takes visitors through the different rooms of the exhibition and back to where they started. Between the entrance and the exit there is a gentle hubbub and mingling of people, some wondering what they are about to see, others wondering how to make sense of what they have seen. It is another of those liminal spaces to notice and pause within, where the beginning and the end look the same, but where we all have a different sense of what it means to be there.

There is an echo here for me in the Terry Pratchett quotation I mentioned earlier, the one I share with our delegates at the opening of every LBCambridge programme at Queens' College:

"Why do you go away? So that you can come back. So that you can see the place you came from with new eyes and extra colours… And the people there see you differently, too. Coming back to where you started is not the same as never leaving."

I love the idea of finding extra colours, but also of coming back to the place we started from. I would therefore like to bring us back to the beginning of this exhibition, because now we are at the end, coming back to the beginning feels very different to when we started, and is definitely not the same as never leaving.

In Chapter One you found me walking into a Baker Street café to meet a man called Lawrence. Now, nearly twenty-three years later, I have just parked in front of a café at the edge of a Cotswold village for another meeting with Lawrence.

The Old Prison Café at Northleach, nestled between Bourton-on-the-Water and Chedworth in the valley of the River Leach, serves fancy artisan coffees, and crucially for Lawrence and me, a beltingly good Old Spot hot sausage roll. The café building, dating from the 1790's, was once a small prison and visitors today can still view the original courtroom and the cells that housed inmates prior to trial. The Old Prison is one of our regular meeting places where we can discuss projects and events; meetings which, over the years, may have become less about our strategic output and more about the quality of the breakfast input.

Working with someone for nearly twenty-three years and speaking with them nearly every day, is not very usual these days. Even more unusual, I think, is that in all that time Lawrence and I have never had a cross word, and never disagreed on what we wanted to do or how we wanted to do it. We have challenged each other's thinking, changed our minds as a result, and worked hard to give every idea a fighting chance, but we have always found the way forward and committed ourselves to it.

I would like to say that we are a true partnership, but to be honest the word "partnership" does not feel precious enough and seems too transactional for the way we work. Lawrence is and always will be so much more than a business partner, and even more than a dear and precious friend.

My mum summed up Lawrence better than I ever will. She used to say to me when we were flying off to South Africa or to the US, or other far-flung places, "Is Lawrence going with you? I always want Lawrence to be with you, he is your guardian angel."

I will struggle to convey the depth of my respect and love for Lawrence. He is the most extraordinary person I have ever worked with. Every week he will say something or do something that will make me stop in my tracks at his thoughtfulness, kindness and creativity. His judgement and resourcefulness are superpowers he carries so lightly, that it would be possible for some people to miss the care, ingenuity and the profoundly important difference he makes, but it also means he sees more, hears more, and does more.

When Lawrence says, "we are all just passing through", it isn't so that we should care less about what we do, but that we should care less for how we let thins affect us. No one I have ever met could care more than Lawrence about doing the best possible work at all times, and his attention to every possible detail is extraordinary; but he also knows not to dwell waiting for validation or vindication, and so he moves on to find the next person to help, the next problem to solve and the next team to make better.

I know that without Lawrence there would never have been an event like LBCambridge (or, therefore, all the other events we have created together since). Indeed, if you recall my meeting with him in the Baker Street café, my career as a consultant, mentor and presenter would not have survived contact with my first client. He has been, and I hope he always well be, a guiding light in my life.

Without Lawrence's Baker Street intervention, I suspect I would have drifted back into just another corporate role, and I may have fallen into that slightly entitled, slightly complacent place where it would have been tempting to settle for comfortable mediocrity. Instead, I have had an extraordinary adventure working with amazing people across the world and travelling to places I didn't even dream of seeing as a small boy in a small town wondering how on earth I would ever make my way in the world.

Lawrence gave me permission to be myself and then backfilled like crazy to make sure our ideas could become real. He protected me, lifted me and encouraged me whenever doubt, or fear or sadness fell into my path. My mum was absolutely right, he is indeed my guardian angel.

So, here I am at the Old Prison Café on 29 August 2023, and the Old Spot sausage rolls are ordered; we're meeting to plan the final details for the next LBCambridge programme in September, the thirty-first time we have held the event.

Before we get to that part of our agenda we have our standard preliminary check-in on the latest adventures with Lawrence's grandchildren, the weekend football and all manner of other world affecting strategic stuff as befits such a high-powered BIG meeting.

However this time, unusually, I sense there a slight hesitation in Lawrence's manner, and then he says, "I've been thinking bud, I think this Cambridge will be my last. It's time to stop. Let's make it a special one, but I will be done when it's over."

I have always known this time would come. We have talked for a few years about what would happen if either of us wanted to stop. Covid nearly killed the business in 2020, and it has been a huge effort to bring it back; we could easily have packed it away then, but we didn't. And I am so proud that we showed the world there was even more meaning in our work after all that everyone had been through in those terrible dark days of the pandemic.

But now the end has arrived in a few short words from Lawrence, and I don't quite have the words to say to him what should be said.

What I think I said in reply, but maybe it is what I hope I said, is, "that's brilliant my friend. I think you are right, we have done enough, but I am so pleased we get to do one more event together."

We began the story twenty-three years ago in one café and we finish the story in another. The exit is next to the entrance, a circular path through amazing adventures, where we shared kindness, friendship and joy in every day.

"Why do we go away?" asked Terry Pratchett; to which I can answer emphatically, so that we can come back. So that we can see the place we came from with new eyes and different colours. Coming back to where we started is not the same as never leaving.

I wasn't sure, at the start of this story, how the exhibition would end. Typically, it seems, I started something that I didn't know how to finish without Lawrence showing me the way.

We are indeed all passing through, and there will be wonderful new adventures for us both, and new stories to tell in the months and years to come. However, what I want you to know most of all right now, is that when Lawrence said he wanted to stop, it was the first and only time in twenty-three years, from Baker Street to The Old Prison Café, that he has asked of me something for himself.

How could I possibly be sad or disappointed.

And what an absolute blast we have had finding extra colours as we were just passing through.

Take care.

With love. Paul xx

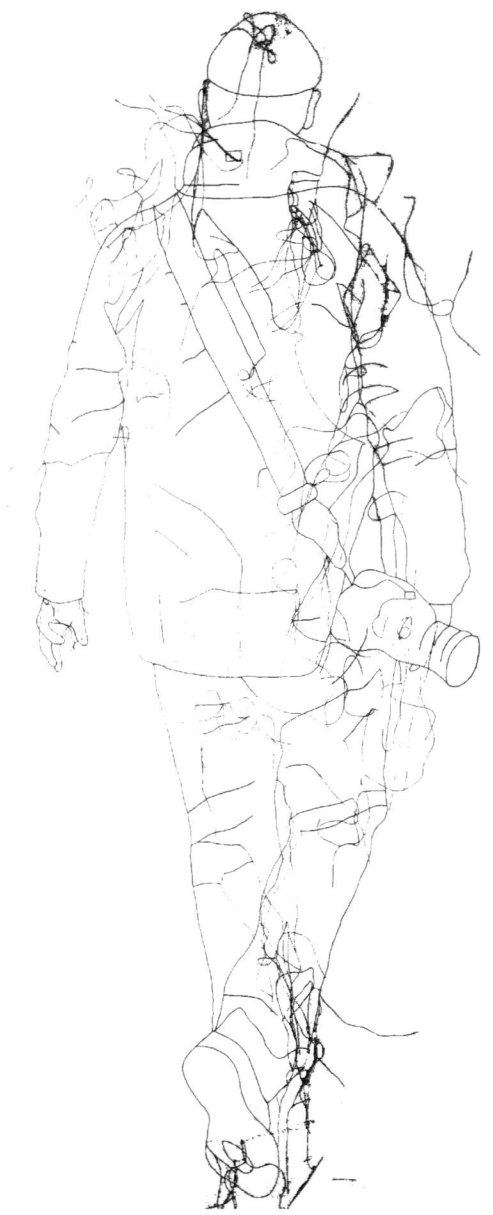

ACKNOWLEDGEMENTS AND THANKS

I am indebted to Jon Honeyford for his skills and care demonstrated throughout this book. Apart from helping to set out the book and designing the cover, many of the images appearing in the book have been created by him, adding considerably to the joy I have found in writing the words.

The montage image of Paul's things and the image of Paul as The Mentor were created by Clive Rose, based on Clive's original photography.

An index of all images in this book appears on the following pages.

This book was originally written as a series of weekly blogs published by Paul on the LBC Wise Counsel website between January and December 2023. We are aware of a small number of typos in those blogs, but Paul has decided not to correct them when bringing the words together in this book. Mistakes made at the time should not be airbrushed from our lives. Every typo you find is just a small reminder that we are fallible and therefore wonderful xx

- A few quiet words — Paul Gilbert
- Wise Counsel — The collected articles of Paul Gilbert
- Carry Each Other — Paul Gilbert
- You are the architect of your future, not the tenant of your past — Paul Gilbert
- The tale of the old badger, the young fox and the wise owl — Paul Gilbert
- A time to care — Paul Gilbert
- One prick to burst a bubble... and other articles by Paul Gilbert
- A butterfly landing on your shoulder — Paul Gilbert

INDEX OF IMAGES

Pages after dedication – a photograph of some of Paul's personal possessions by Clive Rose.

P14 'What? So what? Now What?' – an original image by Jon Honeyford

P19 Tesco bag – an original image by Jon Honeyford

P25 Cover design for Paul's book 'You are the architect...' an original painting by Jon Honeyford

P28 'Janet's tissue' - image generated by DALL-E (OpenAI) and modified by Jon Honeyford using Photoshop

P34-35 Shibuya Crossing photograph by Ryoji Iwata on Unsplash

P36 Paul's admission certificate

P44 Theatre poster for 'Death of a Salesman', reproduced with the kind permission Granger, NYC/ Alamy stock photo

P52 'The Yellow House' van Gogh, reproduced with the kind permission of the van Gogh Museum, Amsterdam

P58 'Steps and ties', an original image by Jon Honeyford

P62 'Sacred Heart' by Jeff Kloons, photograph by Paul

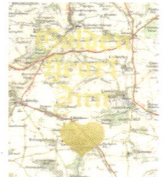

P71 An overlay on a 7th Series, 1952-1973 OS map

170

P75 Photograph of Paul's mum, nan, sister Poppy and brother Jon

P80 Cover image by Jon Honeyford for 'A Few Quiet Words', a book by Paul

P82 The LBC1 and LBC2 Faculty an original image by Jon Honeyford

P89 'The Tree of Life' by Gustav Klimt, reproduced with the kind permission ICP/Alamy stock photo

P90 'Cambridge Colleges' by Iain Weatherhead, original painting commissioned by Paul to be the cover art for LBC1

P96 Generic frame image modified for this book by Jon Honeyford

P102 Butterfly image by Jon Honeyford for 'A butterfly landing on your shoulder', a book by Paul

P108 'Scales of Justice' an original image by Jon Honeyford

P114 'Make others look good' an original image by Jon Honeyford

P120 'Nature makes my heart sing', by Julia Noble, reproduced with the kind permission of Julia

P123 'No one ever says Ray who' an original image by Jon Honeyford

P126 'The Pause' an original image by Jon Honeyford

P132 'Shattered' a drypoint etching on paper by Sam Hodge, reproduced with the kind permission of Sam

P138 'Paul's books' an original image by Jon Honeyford and the cover design by Jon for 'A time to care' by Paul

P142 'Carolyn' an original image by Jon Honeyford

P145 'The bench' photograph by Lawrence Smith

P150 'Carry Each Other' photograph by Lawrence Smith for cover of Paul's book of the same name

P159 'Café sign' an original image by Jon Honeyford

P167 'Lawrence' embroidery image of Lawrence Smith by Christine Smith

P169 'Paul's books' an original image by Jon Honeyford

'The Mentor' an original image by Clive Rose

www.ingramcontent.com/pod-product-compliance
Lightning Source LLC
Chambersburg PA
CBRC100223100526
44590CB00009B/149